BE YOUR OWN SUNSHINE

BE YOUR OWN SUNSHINE

Towards a better tomorrow

JAMES ALLEN

Srishti
PUBLISHERS & DISTRIBUTORS

Srishti Publishers & Distributors
Registered Office: N-16, C.R. Park
New Delhi – 110 019
Corporate Office: 212A, Peacock Lane
Shahpur Jat, New Delhi – 110 049
editorial@srishtipublishers.com

First published by
Srishti Publishers & Distributors in 2020

10 9 8 7 6 5 4 3 2 1

Contents

Introduction

Don't we all know how the world around us moves at a faster pace each day! People, things, situations, emotions and even love get severely complicated in that rush, making it nearly impossible to walk in line with it. Have you ever wondered why it is so important to walk along the world? Why can we not set our own pace, as per our comfort? What happens when we are buried under the fear of being left behind?

These problems may sound contemporary, but have manifested themselves in one form or the other since time immemorial. A definitive way to beat this fear and take control of our lives is to strengthen the mind and the thoughts it generates. This book is a collection of four works that sum up the hows, whys and whats of taming the mind and its infinite energies, of channelizing the power of positive thinking, and striking a balance between the inner world of our thoughts as against the outer world of action.

As A Man Thinketh clearly maps out the way in which our thoughts can affect our physical, mental, emotional and social health. It also discusses ways in which we can use our visions and ideas to lead us to peace of mind. *From Passion to Peace* is a step by step discussion on conquering the factors within us that hinder us from achieving success. *Man: King of Mind, Body and Circumstance* aims at freeing us from the slavery of our negative and binding thoughts, enabling us to conquer our inhibitions and set our spirit free. *Foundation Stones to Happiness and Success* helps us lay the foundation for a stronger self, with the right balance of thoughts, speech and its implementation in action.

James Allen pioneers in the field of motivational literature, as he has mastered the art of amalgamating philosophy and inspiration, with solutions to everyday problems. His writings were greatly philosophical, and at the same time full of positive energy. These handpicked jewels from his pen are an asset for the mind.

AS A MAN THINKETH

Mind is the master power that moulds and makes,
And Man is Mind, and evermore he takes
The tool of Thought, and, shaping what he wills,
Brings forth a thousand joys, a thousand ills:
He thinks in secret, and it comes to pass
Environment is but his looking-glass.

Foreword

This little volume (the result of meditation and experience) is not intended as an exhaustive treatise on the much-written-upon subject of the power of thought. It is suggestive rather than explanatory, its object being to stimulate men and women to the discovery and perception of the truth that –

"They themselves are makers of themselves."

– by virtue of the thoughts, which they choose and encourage; that mind is the master-weaver, both of the inner garment of character and the outer garment of circumstance, and that, as they may have hitherto woven in ignorance and pain they may now weave in enlightenment and happiness.

James Allen

1

Thought and Character

The aphorism, "As a man thinketh in his heart so is he," not only embraces the whole of a man's being, but is so comprehensive as to reach out to every condition and circumstance of his life. A man is literally *what he thinks*, his character being the complete sum of all his thoughts.

As the plant springs from, and could not be without the seed, so every act of a man springs from the hidden seeds of thought, and could not have appeared without them. This applies equally to those acts called "spontaneous" and "unpremeditated" as to those, which are deliberately executed.

Act is the blossom of thought, and joy and suffering are its fruits; thus does a man garner in the sweet and bitter fruitage of his own husbandry.

"Thought in the mind hath made us, What we are
By thought was wrought and built. If a man's mind
Hath evil thoughts, pain comes on him as comes
The wheel the ox behind....
...If one endure
In purity of thought, joy follows him
As his own shadow – sure."

Man is a growth by law, and not a creation by artifice, and cause and effect is as absolute and undeviating in the hidden realm of thought as in the world of visible and material things. A noble and godlike character is not a thing of favour or chance, but is the natural result of continued effort in right thinking, the effect of long-cherished association with godlike thoughts. An ignoble and bestial character, by the same process, is the result of the continued harbouring of grovelling thoughts.

Man is made or unmade by himself. He forges the weapons by which he destroys himself in the armoury of thoughts; he also fashions the tools with which he builds for himself heavenly mansions of joy and strength and peace. By the right choice and true application of thought, man ascends to Divine Perfection. By the abuse and wrong application of thought, he descends below the level of the beast. Between these two extremes are all the grades of character, and man is their maker and master.

Of all the beautiful truths pertaining to the soul which have been restored and brought to light in this age, none is more gladdening or fruitful of divine promise and confidence than this – *that man is the master of thought, the moulder of character, and the maker and shaper of condition, environment, and destiny.*

As a being of Power, Intelligence and Love, and the lord of his own thoughts, man holds the key to every situation, and contains within himself that transforming and regenerative agency by which he may make himself what he wills.

Man is always the master, even in his weaker and most abandoned state; but in his weakness and degradation he is the foolish master who misgoverns his "household". When he begins to reflect upon his condition, and to search diligently for the law upon which his being is established, he then becomes the wise master, directing his energies with intelligence, and fashioning his thoughts to fruitful issues. Such is the *conscious* master, and man can only thus become by discovering *within himself* the laws of thought. This discovery is totally a matter of application, self analysis, and experience.

Only by much searching and mining are gold and diamonds obtained, and man can find every truth connected with his being if he will dig deep into the mine of his soul. He is the maker of his character, the moulder of his life, and the builder of his destiny – he may unerringly prove, if he will watch, control, and alter his thoughts, tracing their effects upon himself, upon others, and upon his life and circumstances, linking cause and effect by patient practice and investigation, and utilizing his every experience, even to the most trivial, everyday occurrence, as a means of obtaining that knowledge of himself which is Understanding, Wisdom, Power. In this direction, as in no other, is the law absolute that "He that seeketh findeth; and to him that knocketh it shall be opened." Only by patience, practice, and ceaseless importunity can a man enter the door of the temple of knowledge.

2

Effect of Thought on Circumstances

Man's mind may be likened to a garden, which may be intelligently cultivated or allowed to run wild; but whether cultivated or neglected, it must, and will, *bring forth*. If no useful seeds are *put* into it, then an abundance of useless weed-seeds will *fall* therein, and will continue to produce their kind.

Just as a gardener cultivates his plot, keeping it free from weeds, and growing the flowers and fruits which he requires, so may a man tend the garden of his mind, weeding out all the wrong, useless, and impure thoughts, and cultivating toward perfection the flowers and fruits of right, useful, and pure thoughts. By pursuing this process, a man sooner or later discovers that he is the master-gardener of his soul, the director of his life. He also reveals, within himself, the laws of thought, and understands, with ever-increasing accuracy, how the thought-forces and mind elements operate in the shaping of his character, circumstances, and destiny.

Thought and character are one, and as character can only manifest and discover itself through environment and circumstance, the outer conditions of a person's life will always be found to be harmoniously related to his inner state. This does not mean that a man's circumstances at any given time are an indication of his *entire* character, but that those circumstances are so intimately connected with some vital thought-element within himself that for the time being, they are indispensable to his development.

Every man is where he is by the law of his being; the thoughts which he has built into his character have brought him there. In the arrangement of his life, there is no element of chance, but all is the result of a law which cannot err. This is just as true of those who feel "out of harmony" with their surroundings as of those who are contented with them.

As a progressive and evolving being, man is where he is that he may learn that he may grow; and as he learns the spiritual lesson which any circumstance contains for him, it passes away and gives place to other circumstances.

Man is buffeted by circumstances so long as he believes himself to be the creature of outside conditions. But when he realizes that he is a creative power, and that he may command the hidden soil and seeds of his being out of which circumstances grow, he then becomes the rightful master of himself.

That circumstances grow out of thought every man knows who has for any length of time practised self-control and self-purification, for he will have noticed that the alteration in his circumstances has been in exact ratio with his altered mental condition. So true is this that when a man earnestly applies himself to remedy the defects in his character, and makes swift and marked progress, he passes rapidly through a succession of vicissitudes.

The soul attracts that which it secretly harbours; that which it loves, and also that which it fears; it reaches the height of its cherished aspirations; it falls to the level of its unchastened desires – and circumstances are the means by which the soul receives its own.

Every thought-seed sown or allowed to fall into the mind, and to take root there, produces its own, blossoming sooner or later into act, and bearing its own fruitage of opportunity and circumstance. Good thoughts bear good fruit; bad thoughts bear bad fruit.

The outer world of circumstance shapes itself to the inner world of thought, and both pleasant and unpleasant external conditions are factors, which make for the ultimate good of the individual. As the reaper of his own harvest, man learns both by suffering and bliss.

Following the inmost desires, aspirations, thoughts, by which he allows himself to be dominated, a man at last arrives at their fruition and fulfilment in the outer conditions of his life. The laws of growth and adjustment obtains everywhere.

A man does not come to the almshouse or the jail by the tyranny of fate or circumstance, but by the pathway of grovelling thoughts and base desires. Nor does a pure-minded man fall suddenly into crime by stress of any mere external force; the criminal thought had long been secretly fostered in the heart, and the hour of opportunity revealed its gathered power. Circumstance does not make the man; it reveals him to himself. No such conditions can exist as descending into vice and its attendant sufferings apart from vicious inclinations, or ascending into virtue and its pure happiness without the continued cultivation of virtuous aspirations. And man, therefore, as the lord and master of thought, is the maker of himself the shaper and author of environment. Even at birth the soul comes to its own and through every step of its earthly pilgrimage, it attracts those combinations of conditions which reveal itself, which are the reflections of its own purity and impurity, its strength and weakness.

Men do not attract that which they *want*, but that which they *are*. Their whims, fancies, and ambitions are thwarted at every step, but their inmost thoughts and desires are fed with their own food, be it foul or clean. The "divinity that shapes our ends" is in ourselves; it is our very self. Only himself manacles man. Thought and action are the jailors of fate – they imprison, being base; they are also the angels of freedom – they liberate, being noble. The man does not get what he wishes and prays for, but what he justly earns. His wishes and prayers are only gratified and answered when they harmonize with his thoughts and actions.

In the light of this truth, what then is the meaning of "fighting against circumstances"? It means that a man is continually revolting against an *effect* without, while all the time he is nourishing and preserving its *cause* in his heart. That cause may take the form of a conscious vice or an unconscious weakness; but whatever it is, it stubbornly retards the efforts of its possessor, and thus calls aloud for remedy.

Men are anxious to improve their circumstances, but are unwilling to improve themselves; they therefore remain bound. The man who does not shrink from self-crucifixion can never fail to accomplish the object upon which his heart is set. This is as true of earthly as of heavenly things. Even the man whose sole object is to acquire wealth must be prepared to make great personal sacrifices before he can accomplish his object; and how much more so he who would realize a strong and well-poised life?

Here is a man who is wretchedly poor. He is extremely anxious that his surroundings and home comforts should be improved, yet all the time he shirks his work, and considers he is justified in trying to deceive his employer on the ground of the insufficiency of his wages. Such a man does not understand the simplest rudiments of those principles which are the basis of true prosperity. He is not only totally unfitted to rise out of his wretchedness, but is actually attracting to himself a still deeper wretchedness by dwelling in, and acting out, indolent, deceptive, and unmanly thoughts.

Here is a rich man who is the victim of a painful and persistent disease as the result of gluttony. He is willing to give large sums of money to get rid of it, but he will not sacrifice his gluttonous desires. He wants to gratify his taste for rich and unnatural viands and have his health as well. Such a man is totally unfit to have health, because he has not yet learned the first principles of a healthy life.

Here is an employer of labour who adopts crooked measures to avoid paying the regulation wage, and, in the hope of making larger profits, reduces the wages of his workpeople. Such a man is altogether unfitted for prosperity, and when he finds himself bankrupt, both as regards reputation and riches, he blames circumstances, not knowing that he is the sole author of his condition.

I have introduced these three cases merely as illustrative of the truth that man is the causer (though nearly always is unconsciously) of his circumstances, and that, while aiming at a good end, he is continually frustrating its accomplishment by encouraging thoughts and desires which cannot possibly harmonize with that end. Such cases could be multiplied and varied almost indefinitely, but this is not necessary, as the reader can, if he so resolves, trace the action of the laws of thought in his own mind and life, and until this is done, mere external facts cannot serve as a ground of reasoning.

Circumstances, however, are so complicated, thought is so deeply rooted, and the conditions of happiness vary so vastly with individuals, that a man's entire soul-condition (although it may be known to himself) cannot be judged by another from the external aspect of his life alone. A man may be honest in certain directions, yet suffer privations; a man may be dishonest in certain directions, yet acquire wealth; but the conclusion usually formed that the one man fails *because of his particular honesty*, and that the other *prospers because of his particular dishonesty*, is the result of a superficial judgment, which assumes that the dishonest man is almost totally corrupt, and the honest man almost entirely virtuous. In the light of a deeper knowledge and wider experience, such judgment is found to be erroneous. The dishonest man may have some admirable virtues, which the other does not possess; and the honest man obnoxious vices, which are absent in the other. The honest man reaps the good results of his honest thoughts and acts; he also brings upon himself the sufferings, which his vices produce. The dishonest man likewise garners his own suffering and happiness.

It is pleasing to human vanity to believe that one suffers because of one's virtue; but not until a man has extirpated every sickly, bitter, and impure thought from his mind, and washed every sinful stain from his soul, can he be in a position to know and declare that his sufferings are the result of his good, and not of his bad qualities. On the way to, yet long before he has reached, that supreme perfection, he will have found, working in his mind and life, the Great Law which is absolutely just, and which cannot, therefore, give good for evil, evil for good. Possessed of such knowledge, he will then know, looking back upon his past ignorance and blindness, that his life is, and always was, justly ordered, and that all his past experiences, good and bad, were the equitable outworking of his evolving, yet unevolved self.

Good thoughts and actions can never produce bad results; bad thoughts and actions can never produce good results. This is but saying that nothing can come from corn but corn, nothing from nettles but nettles. Men understand this law in the natural world, and work with it; but few understand it in the mental and moral world (though its operation there is just as simple and undeviating), and they, therefore, do not co-operate with it.

Suffering is *always* the effect of wrong thought in some direction. It is an indication that the individual is out of harmony with himself, with the law of his being. The sole and supreme use of suffering is to purify, to burn out all that is useless and impure. Suffering ceases for him who is pure. There could be no object in burning gold after the dross had been removed, and a perfectly pure and enlightened being could not suffer.

The circumstances, which a man encounters with suffering, are the result of his own mental inharmony. The circumstances, which a man encounters with blessedness, are the result of his own mental harmony. Blessedness, not material possessions, is the measure of right thought. Wretchedness, not lack of material possessions, is the measure of wrong thought. A man may be cursed and rich; he may be blessed and poor. Blessedness and riches are only joined together when the riches are rightly and wisely used; and the poor man only descends into wretchedness when he regards his lot as a burden unjustly imposed.

Indigence and indulgence are the two extremes of wretchedness. They are both equally unnatural and the result of mental disorder. A man is not rightly conditioned until he is a happy, healthy, and prosperous being; and happiness, health, and prosperity are the result of a harmonious adjustment of the inner with the outer, of the man with his surroundings.

A man only begins to be a man when he ceases to whine and revile, and commences to search for the hidden justice which regulates his life. And as he adapts his mind to that regulating factor, he ceases to accuse others as the cause of his condition, and builds himself up in strong and noble thoughts. He ceases to kick against circumstances, but begins to *use* them as aids to his more rapid progress, and as a means of discovering the hidden powers and possibilities within himself.

Law, not confusion, is the dominating principle in the universe; justice, not injustice, is the soul and substance of life; and righteousness, not corruption, is the moulding and moving force in the spiritual government of the world. This being so, man has but to right himself to find that the universe is right. During the process of putting himself right, he will find that as he alters his thoughts towards things and other people, things and other people will alter towards him.

The proof of this truth is in every person, and it therefore admits of easy investigation by systematic introspection and self-analysis. Let a man radically alter his thoughts, and he will be astonished at the rapid transformation it will effect in the material conditions of his life. Men imagine that thought can be kept secret, but it cannot; it rapidly crystallizes into habit, and habit solidifies into circumstance. Bestial thoughts crystallize into habits of drunkenness and sensuality, which solidify into circumstances of destitution and disease. Just like impure thoughts of every kind crystallize into enervating and confusing habits, which solidify into distracting and adverse circumstances. Thoughts of fear, doubt, and indecision crystallize into weak, unmanly, and irresolute habits, which solidify into circumstances of failure, indigence, and slavish dependence. Further, lazy thoughts crystallize into habits of uncleanliness and dishonesty, which solidify into circumstances of foulness and beggary. Hateful and condemnatory thoughts crystallize into habits of accusation and violence, which solidify into circumstances of injury and persecution. Similarly, selfish thoughts of all kinds crystallize into habits of self-seeking, which solidify into circumstances more or less distressing. On the other hand, beautiful thoughts of all kinds crystallize into habits of grace and kindliness, which solidify into genial and sunny circumstances. For instance, pure thoughts crystallize into habits of temperance and self-control, which solidify into circumstances of repose and peace. Thoughts of courage, self-reliance and decision crystallize into manly habits, which solidify into circumstances of success, plenty, and freedom. Energetic thoughts crystallize into habits of cleanliness and industry, which solidify into circumstances of pleasantness. Gentle and forgiving thoughts crystallize into habits of gentleness, which solidify into protective and preservative circumstances. Loving and unselfish thoughts crystallize into habits of self-forgetfulness for others, which solidify into circumstances of sure and abiding prosperity, and true riches.

A particular train of thought persisted in, be it good or bad, cannot fail to produce its results on the character and circumstances. A man cannot *directly* choose his circumstances, but he can choose his thoughts, and so indirectly, yet surely, shape his circumstances.

Nature helps every man to the gratification of the thoughts, which he most encourages, and opportunities are presented which will most speedily bring to the surface both the good and evil thoughts.

Let a man cease from his sinful thoughts, and all the world will soften towards him, and be ready to help him. Let him put away his weakly and sickly thoughts, and lo, opportunities will spring up on every hand to aid his strong resolves. Let him encourage good thoughts, and no hard fate shall bind him down to wretchedness and shame. The world is your kaleidoscope, and the varying combinations of colours, which at every succeeding moment it presents to you, are the exquisitely adjusted pictures of your ever-moving thoughts.

"So you will be what you will to be;
Let failure find its false content
In that poor word, 'environment,'
But spirit scorns it, and is free.

It masters time, it conquers space;
It cowes that boastful trickster, Chance,
And bids the tyrant Circumstance
Uncrown, and fill a servant's place.

The human Will, that force unseen,
The offspring of a deathless Soul,
Can hew a way to any goal,
Though walls of granite intervene.

Be not impatient in delays
But wait as one who understands;
When spirit rises and commands
The gods are ready to obey."

3

Effect of Thought on Health and the Body

The body is the servant of the mind. It obeys the operations of the mind, whether they be deliberately chosen or automatically expressed. At the bidding of unlawful thoughts, the body sinks rapidly into disease and decay; at the command of glad and beautiful thoughts, it becomes clothed with youthfulness and beauty.

Disease and health, like circumstances, are rooted in thought. Sickly thoughts will express themselves through a sickly body. Thoughts of fear have been known to kill a man as speedily as a bullet, and they are continually killing thousands of people just as surely, though less rapidly. The people who live in fear of disease are the people who get it. Anxiety quickly demoralizes the whole body, and lays it open to disease; while impure thoughts, even if not physically indulged, will soon shatter the nervous system.

Strong, pure and happy thoughts build up the body in vigour and grace. The body is a delicate and plastic instrument, which responds readily to the thoughts by which it is impressed, and habits of thought will produce their own effects, good or bad, upon it.

Men will continue to have impure and poisoned blood, so long as they propagate unclean thoughts. Out of a clean heart comes a clean life and a clean body. Out of a defiled mind proceeds a defiled life and a corrupt body. Thought is the fount of action, life and manifestation; make the fountain pure, and all will be pure.

Change of diet will not help a man who will not change his thoughts. When a man makes his thoughts pure, he no longer desires impure food.

Clean thoughts make clean habits. The so-called saint who does not wash his body is not a saint. He who has strengthened and purified his thoughts does not need to consider the malevolent microbe.

Like you would protect your body, guard your mind. If you would renew your body, beautify your mind. Thoughts of malice, envy, disappointment and despondency rob the body of its health and grace. A sour face does not come by chance; it is made by sour thoughts. Wrinkles that mar are drawn by folly, passion and pride.

I know a woman of ninety-six who has the bright, innocent face of a girl. I know a man well under middle age whose face is drawn into inharmonious contours. The one is the result of a sweet and sunny disposition; the other is the outcome of passion and discontent.

As you cannot have a sweet and wholesome abode unless you admit the air and sunshine freely into your rooms, so a strong body and a bright, happy or serene countenance can only result from the free admittance into the mind of thoughts of joy, goodwill and serenity.

On the faces of the aged there are wrinkles made by sympathy, others by strong and pure thought, and others are carved by passion: who cannot distinguish them? With those who have lived righteously, age is calm, peaceful, and softly mellowed, like the setting sun. I have recently seen a philosopher on his deathbed. He was not old except in years. He died as sweetly and peacefully as he had lived.

There is no physician like cheerful thought for dissipating the ills of the body; there is no comforter to compare with goodwill for dispersing the shadows of grief and sorrow. To live continually in thoughts of ill will, cynicism, suspicion, and envy, is to be confined in a self made prison-hole. But to think well of all, to be cheerful with all, to patiently learn to find the good in all – such unselfish thoughts are the very portals of heaven. To dwell day by day in thoughts of peace toward every creature will bring abounding peace to their possessor.

4

Thought and Purpose

Until thought is linked with purpose there is no intelligent accomplishment. With the majority, the bark of thought is allowed to "drift" upon the ocean of life. Aimlessness is a vice, and such drifting must not continue for him who would steer clear of catastrophe and destruction.

Those who have no central purpose in their life fall an easy prey to petty worries, fears, troubles and self-pitying, all of which are indications of weakness, which lead, just as surely as deliberately planned sins (though by a different route), to failure, unhappiness and loss, for weakness cannot persist in a power evolving universe.

A man should conceive of a legitimate purpose in his heart, and set out to accomplish it. He should make this purpose the centralizing point of his thoughts. It may take the form of a spiritual ideal, or it may be a worldly object, according to his nature at the time being; but whichever it is, he should steadily focus his thought-forces upon the object, which he has set before him. He should make this purpose his supreme duty, and should devote himself to its attainment, not allowing his thoughts to wander away into ephemeral fancies, longings and imaginings. This is the royal road to self-control and true concentration of thought. Even if he fails again and again to accomplish his purpose (as he necessarily must until weakness is overcome), the *strength of character gained* will be the measure of his true success, and this will form a new starting-point for future power and triumph.

Those who are not prepared for the apprehension of a *great* purpose should fix the thoughts upon the faultless performance of their duty, no matter how insignificant their task may appear. Only in this way can the thoughts be gathered and focussed, and resolution and energy be developed, which being done, there is nothing which may not be accomplished.

The weakest soul, knowing its own weakness, and believing this truth 'that strength can only be developed by effort and practice, *will, thus believing, at once begin to exert itself, and adding effort to effort, patience to patience, and strength to strength, will never cease to develop, and will at last grow divinely strong.*

As the physically weak man can make himself strong by careful and patient training, so the man of weak thoughts can make himself strong by exercising himself in right thinking.

To put away aimlessness and weakness, and to begin to think with purpose, is to enter the ranks of those strong ones who only recognize failure as one of the pathways to attainment; who make all conditions serve them, and who think strongly, attempt fearlessly, and accomplish masterfully.

Having conceived of his purpose, a man should mentally mark out a *straight* pathway to its achievement, looking neither to the right nor the left. Doubts and fears should be rigorously excluded; they are disintegrating elements, which break up the straight line of effort, rendering it crooked, ineffectual, useless. Thoughts of doubt and fear never accomplished anything, and never can. They always lead to failure. Purpose, energy, power to do and all strong thoughts cease when doubt and fear creep in.

The will to do springs from the knowledge that we *can* do. Doubt and fear are the great enemies of knowledge, and he who encourages them, who does not slay them, thwarts himself at every step.

He who has conquered doubt and fear has conquered failure. His every thought is allied with power, and all difficulties are bravely met and wisely overcome. His purposes are seasonably planted, and they bloom and bring forth fruit, which does not fall prematurely to the ground.

Thought allied fearlessly to purpose becomes creative force: he who *knows* this is ready to become something higher and stronger than a mere bundle of wavering thoughts and fluctuating sensations; he who *does* this has become the conscious and intelligent wielder of his mental powers.

5

The Thought-Factor in Achievement

All that a man achieves and all that he fails to achieve is the direct result of his own thoughts. In a justly ordered universe, where loss of equipoise would mean total destruction, individual responsibility must be absolute. A man's weakness and strength, purity and impurity, are his own, and not another man's; they are brought about by himself, and not by another; and they can only be altered by himself, never by another. His condition is also his own, and not another man's. His suffering and his happiness are evolved from within. As he thinks, so he is; as he continues to think, so he remains.

A strong man cannot help a weaker unless that weaker is *willing* to be helped, and even then the weak man must become strong of himself; he must, by his own efforts, develop the strength which he admires in another. None but himself can alter his condition.

It has been usual for men to think and to say, "Many men are slaves because one is an oppressor; let us hate the oppressor." Now, however, there is amongst an increasing few a tendency to reverse this judgment, and to say, "One man is an oppressor because many are slaves; let us despise the slaves."

The truth is that oppressor and slave are co-operators in ignorance, and, while seeming to afflict each other, are in reality afflicting themselves. A perfect knowledge perceives the action of law in the weakness of the oppressed and the misapplied power of the oppressor; a perfect love, seeing the suffering, which both states entail, condemns neither; a perfect compassion embraces both oppressor and oppressed.

He who has conquered weakness, and has put away all selfish thoughts, belongs neither to oppressor nor oppressed. He is free.

A man can only rise, conquer, and achieve by lifting up his thoughts. He can only remain weak, abject and miserable by refusing to lift up his thoughts.

Before a man can achieve anything, even in worldly things, he must lift his thoughts above slavish animal indulgence. He may not, in order to succeed, give up all animality and selfishness, by any means; but a portion of it must, at least, be sacrificed. A man whose first thought is bestial indulgence could neither think clearly nor plan methodically; he could not find and develop his latent resources, and would fail in any undertaking. Not having commenced to manfully control his thoughts, he is not in a position to control affairs and to adopt serious responsibilities. He is not fit to act independently and stand alone. But he is limited only by the thoughts, which he chooses.

There can be no progress, no achievement without sacrifice, and a man's worldly success will be in the measure that he sacrifices his confused animal thoughts, fixes his mind on the development of his plans, and the strengthening of his resolution and self-reliance. And the higher he lifts his thoughts, the more manly, upright and righteous he becomes, the greater will be his success, the more blessed and enduring will be his achievements.

The universe does not favour the greedy, the dishonest, the vicious, although on the mere surface it may sometimes appear to do so; it helps the honest, the magnanimous, the virtuous. All the great teachers of the ages have declared this in varying forms, and to prove and know it, a man has but to persist in making himself more and more virtuous by lifting up his thoughts.

Intellectual achievements are the result of thought consecrated to the search for knowledge, or for the beautiful and true in life and nature. Such achievements may be sometimes connected with vanity and ambition, but they are not the outcome of those characteristics; they are the natural outgrowth of long and arduous effort, and of pure and unselfish thoughts.

Spiritual achievements are the consummation of holy aspirations. He who lives constantly in the conception of noble and lofty thoughts, who dwells upon all that is pure and unselfish, will, as surely as the sun reaches its zenith and the moon its full, become wise and noble in character, and rise into a position of influence and blessedness.

Achievement, of whatever kind, is the crown of effort, the diadem of thought. By the aid of self-control, resolution, purity, righteousness, and well-directed thought, a man ascends the aid of animality, indolence, impurity, corruption and confusion of thought, a man descends.

A man may rise to high success in the world, and even to lofty altitudes in the spiritual realm, and again descend into weakness and wretchedness by allowing arrogant, selfish, and corrupt thoughts to take possession of him.

Victories attained by right thought can only be maintained by watchfulness. Many give way when success is assured, and rapidly fall back into failure.

All achievements, whether in the business, intellectual, or spiritual world, are the result of definitely directed thought. They are governed by the same law and are of the same method; the only difference lies in *the object of attainment*.

He who would accomplish little must sacrifice little; he who would achieve much must sacrifice much; he who would attain highly must sacrifice greatly.

6

Visions and Ideals

The dreamers are the saviours of the world. As the visible world is sustained by the invisible, so men, through all their trials and sins and sordid vocations, are nourished by the beautiful visions of their solitary dreamers. Humanity cannot forget its dreamers; it cannot let their ideals fade and die; it lives in them; it knows them as they know the *realities* which it shall one day see and know.

Composer, sculptor, painter, poet, prophet, sage – these are the makers of the after-world, the architects of heaven. The world is beautiful because they have lived; without them, labouring humanity would perish.

He who cherishes a beautiful vision, a lofty ideal in his heart, will one day realize it. Columbus cherished a vision of another world, and he discovered it; Copernicus fostered the vision of a multiplicity of worlds and a wider universe, and he revealed it; Buddha beheld the vision of a spiritual world of stainless beauty and perfect peace, and entered into it.

Cherish your visions; cherish your ideals; cherish the music that stirs in your heart, the beauty that forms in your mind, the loveliness that drapes your purest thoughts, for out of them will grow all delightful conditions, all heavenly environment. If you remain true to them, your world will at last be built.

To desire is to obtain; to aspire is to achieve. Shall man's basest desires receive the fullest measure of gratification, and his purest aspirations starve for lack of sustenance? Such is not the law: such a condition of things can never obtain: "ask and receive."

Dream lofty dreams, and as you dream, so shall you become. Your vision is the promise of what you shall one day be; your ideal is the prophecy of what you shall at last unveil.

The greatest achievement was at first and for a time a dream. The oak sleeps in the acorn; the bird waits in the egg; and in the highest vision of the soul, a waking angel stirs. Dreams are the seedlings of realities.

Your circumstances may be uncongenial, but they shall not long remain so if you but perceive an ideal and strive to reach it. You cannot travel *within* and stand still *without*. Here is a youth hard pressed by poverty and labour; confined long hours in an unhealthy workshop; unschooled, and lacking all the arts of refinement. But he dreams of better things; he thinks of intelligence, of refinement, of grace and beauty. He conceives of, mentally builds up, an ideal condition of life; the vision of a wider liberty and a larger scope takes possession of him; unrest urges him to action, and he utilizes all his spare time and means, small though they are, to the development of his latent powers and resources. Very soon, so altered has his mind become that the workshop can no longer hold him. It has become so out of harmony with his mentality that it falls out of his life as a garment is cast aside, and, with the growth of opportunities, which fit the scope of his expanding powers, he passes out of it forever. Years later, we see this youth as a full-grown man. We find him a master of certain forces of the mind, which he wields with worldwide influence and almost unequalled power. In his hands he holds the cords of gigantic responsibilities; he speaks, and lo, lives are changed! Men and women hang upon his words and remould their characters, and, sunlike, he becomes the fixed and luminous centre round which innumerable destinies revolve. He has realized the vision of his youth. He has become one with his ideal.

And you, too, youthful reader, will realize the vision (not the idle wish) of your heart, be it base or beautiful, or a mixture of both, for you will always gravitate toward that which you most love, even if secretly. Into your hands will be placed the exact results of your own thoughts; you will receive that which you earn; no more, no less. Whatever your present environment may be, you will fall, remain, or rise with your thoughts, your vision, your ideal. You will become as small as your controlling desire, and as great as your dominant aspiration. In the beautiful words of Stanton Kirkham Davis, "You may be keeping accounts, and presently you shall walk out of the door that for so long has seemed to you the barrier of your ideals, and shall find yourself before an audience – the pen still behind your ear, the ink stains on your fingers and then and there shall pour out the torrent of your inspiration. You may be driving sheep, and you shall wander to the city-bucolic and open-mouthed; shall wander under the intrepid guidance of the spirit into the studio of the master, and after a time he shall say, 'I have nothing more to teach you'. And now you have become the master, who did so recently dream of great things while driving sheep. You shall lay down the saw and the plane to take upon yourself the regeneration of the world."

The thoughtless, the ignorant, and the indolent, seeing only the apparent effects of things and not the things themselves, talk of luck, fortune and chance. Seeing a man grow rich, they say, "How lucky he is!" Observing another become intellectual, they exclaim, "How highly favoured he is!" And noting the saintly character and wide influence of another, they remark, "How chance aids him at every turn!" They do not see the trials and failures and struggles which these men have voluntarily encountered in order to gain their experience. The ones criticizing have no knowledge of the sacrifices they have made, of the undaunted efforts they have put forth, of the faith they have exercised, that they might overcome the apparently insurmountable, and realize the vision of their heart. They do not know the darkness and the heartaches; they only see the light and joy, and call it "luck". They do not see the long and arduous journey, but only behold the pleasant goal, and call it "good fortune," do not understand the process, but only perceive the result, and call it chance.

In all human affairs there are *efforts*, and there are *results*, and the strength of the effort is the measure of the result. Chance is not. Gifts, powers, material, intellectual, and spiritual possessions are the fruits of effort; they are thoughts completed, objects accomplished, visions realized.

The vision that you glorify in your mind, the ideal that you enthrone in your heart – this you will build your life by, this you will become.

7

Serenity

Calmness of mind is one of the beautiful jewels of wisdom. It is the result of a long and patient effort in self-control. Its presence is an indication of ripened experience, and of a more than ordinary knowledge of the laws and operations of thought.

A man becomes calm in the measure that he understands himself as a thought-evolved being, for such knowledge necessitates the understanding of others as the result of thought, and as he develops a right understanding, and sees more and more clearly the internal relations of things by the action of cause and effect, he ceases to fuss and fume and worry and grieve, and remains poised, steadfast, serene.

The calm man, having learned how to govern himself, knows how to adapt himself to others; and they, in turn, revere his spiritual strength, and feel that they can learn from him and rely upon him. The more tranquil a man becomes, the greater is his success, his influence, his power for good. Even the ordinary trader will find his business prosperity increase as he develops a greater self-control and equanimity, for people will always prefer to deal with a man whose demeanour is strongly equable.

The strong, calm man is always loved and revered. He is like a shade-giving tree in a thirsty land, or a sheltering rock in a storm. "Who does not love a tranquil heart, a sweet-tempered, balanced life? It does not matter whether it rains or shines, or what changes come to those possessing these blessings, for they are always sweet, serene, and calm. That exquisite poise of character, which we call serenity is the last lesson of culture, the fruitage of the soul. It is precious as wisdom, to be desired more than even fine gold. How insignificant mere money seeking looks in comparison with a serene life – a life that dwells in the ocean of truth, beneath the waves, beyond the reach of tempests, in the eternal calm!

"How many people do we know who sour their lives, who ruin all that is sweet and beautiful by explosive tempers, who destroy their poise of character, and make bad blood! It is a question whether the great majority of people do not ruin their lives and mar their happiness by lack of self-control. How few people we meet in life who are well balanced, who have that exquisite poise which is characteristic of the finished character!

Yes, humanity surges with uncontrolled passion, is tumultuous with ungoverned grief, is blown about by anxiety and doubt. Only the wise man, only he whose thoughts are controlled and purified, makes the winds and the storms of the soul obey him.

Tempest-tossed souls, wherever ye may be, under whatsoever conditions ye may live, know this: In the ocean of life the isles of blessedness are smiling, and the sunny shore of your ideal awaits your coming. Keep your hand firmly upon the helm of thought. In the bark of your soul reclines the commanding master. He does but sleep; wake Him. Self-control is strength; Right Thought is mastery; Calmness is power. Say unto your heart, "Peace, be still!"

FROM PASSION TO PEACE

Amid the din and strife of men,
The Call Divine I hear again;
Its telling is of things apart;
Above the tumult of the heart.
High o'er where sin's dark pathways wind
Waits the wise willing of the mind;
Beyond strong Passion's guarded gates,
There Peace awaits – there Peace awaits.

Foreword

The first three parts of this book, *Passion*, *Aspiration*, and *Temptation*, represent the common human life, with its passion, pathos, and tragedy. The last three parts, *Transcendence*, *Beatitude* and *Peace*, represents the divine life – calm, wise and beautiful – of the sage and savior. The middle part, *Transmutation*, is the transitional stage between the two; it is the alchemic process linking the divine with the human life. Discipline, denial, and renunciation do not constitute the divine state; they are only the means by which it is attained. Divine life is established in that perfect knowledge which bestows perfect peace.

James Allen

1

Passion

The pathway of the saints and sages, the road of the wise and the pure, the highway along which the saviors have trod, and which all saviors to come will also walk – such is the subject of this book; such is the high and holy theme which the author briefly expounds in these pages.

Passion is the lowest level of human life. None can descend lower. In its chilling swamps and concealing darkness creep and crawl the creatures of the sunless world. Lust, hatred, anger, covetousness, pride, vanity, greed, revenge, envy, back-biting, lying, theft, deceit, treachery, cruelty, suspicion, jealousy – such are the brute forces and blind, unreasoning impulses that inhabit the underworld of passion, and roam, devouring and devoured, in the rank primeval jungles of the human mind.

There also dwell the dark shapes of remorse, pain, and suffering, and the drooping forms of grief, sorrow, and lamentation.

In this dark world the unwise live and die, not knowing the peace of purity, nor the joy of that divine light which forever shines above them, and for them. Yet, it shines in vain so long as it falls on unseeing eyes which never look up, but are ever bent earthward, fleshward.

But the wise look up. They are not satisfied with this passion-world. They bend their steps towards the upper world of peace, the light and the glory of which they behold, at first far off, but nearer and with ever increasing splendor as they ascend.

None can fall lower than passion, but all can rise higher. In that lowest place where further descent is impossible, all who move forward must ascend. The ascending pathway is always at hand, and easily accessible. It is the way of self-conquest. He has already entered it who has begun to say "nay" to his selfishness, who has begun to discipline his desires, and to control and command the unruly elements of his mind.

Passion is the archenemy of mankind, the slayer of happiness, the opposite and enemy of peace. From it proceeds all that defiles and destroys. It is the source of misery, and the promulgator of mischief and disaster.

The inner world of selfishness is rooted in ignorance – ignorance of divine law, of divine goodness; ignorance of the pure way and the peaceful path. Passion is dark, and it thrives and flourishes in spiritual darkness. It cannot enter the regions of spiritual light. In the enlightened mind the darkness of ignorance is destroyed; in the pure heart there is no place for passion.

Passion in all its forms is a mental thirst, a fever, a torturing unrest. As a fire consumes a magnificent building, reducing it to a heap of unsightly ashes, so are men consumed by the flames of passions, and their deeds and works fall and perish.

If one finds peace, he must come out of passion. The wise man subdues his passions, the foolish man is subdued by them. The seeker for wisdom begins by turning his back on folly. The lover of peace enters the way which leads thereto, and with every step he takes, he leaves further below and behind him the dark dwelling place of passion and despair.

The first step towards the heights of wisdom and peace is to understand the darkness and misery of selfishness, and when that is understood, the overcoming of it – the coming out of it – will follow.

Selfishness, or passion, not only subsists in the gross forms of greed and glaringly ungoverned conditions of mind; it informs also every hidden thought which is subtly connected with the assumption and glorification of one's self. It is most deceiving and subtle when it prompts one to dwell upon the selfishness in others, to accuse them of it and to talk about it. The man who continually dwells upon the selfishness in others will not thus overcome his own selfishness. We do not come out of selfishness by accusing others, but by purifying ourselves.

The way from passion to peace is not by hurling painful charges against others, but by overcoming one's self. By eagerly striving to subdue the selfishness of others, we remain passion-bound. By patiently overcoming our own selfishness, we ascend into freedom. Only he who has conquered himself can subdue others; and he subdues them not by passion, but by love.

The foolish man accuses others and justifies himself, but he who is becoming wise justifies others and accuses himself. The way from passion to peace is not in the outer world of people; it is in the inner world of thoughts. It does not consist in altering the deeds of others, it consists in perfecting one's own deeds.

Frequently, the man of passion is most eager to put others right; but the man of wisdom puts himself right. If one is anxious to reform the world, let him begin by reforming himself. The reformation of self does not end with the elimination of the sensual elements only; that is its beginning. It ends only when every vain thought and selfish aim is overcome. Short of perfect purity and wisdom, there is still some form of self-slavery or folly which needs to be conquered.

Passion is at the base of the structure of life; peace is at its crown and summit. Without passion to begin with, there would be no power to work with, and no achievement to end with. Passion represents power, but if power is misdirected, power ends up producing hurt instead of happiness. Its forces, while instruments of destruction in the hands of the foolish, are instruments of preservation in the hands of the wise. When curbed and concentrated and beneficially directed, they represent working energy. Passion is the flaming sword which guards the gates of paradise. It shuts out and destroys the foolish; it admits and preserves the wise.

He is the foolish man who does not know the extent of his own ignorance; who is the slave of thoughts of self; who obeys the impulses of passion. He is the wise man who knows his own ignorance; who understands the emptiness of selfish thoughts; who masters the impulses of passion.

The fool descends into deeper and deeper ignorance; the wise man ascends into higher and higher knowledge. The fool desires, suffers and dies. The wise man aspires, rejoices, and lives.

With mind intent on wisdom and mental gaze raised upward, the spiritual warrior perceives the upward way, and fixes his attention upon the heights of peace.

2

Aspiration

With the clear perception of one's own ignorance comes the desire for enlightenment, and thus in the heart is born aspiration, the rapture of the saints.

On the wings of aspiration, man rises from earth to heaven, from ignorance to knowledge, from the under darkness to the upper light. Without it he remains a grovelling animal, earthly, sensual, unenlightened and uninspired.

Aspiration is the longing for heavenly things – for righteousness, compassion, purity, love – as distinguished from desire, which is the longing for earthly things – for selfish possessions, personal dominance, low pleasures, and sensual gratifications.

As a bird deprived of its wings cannot soar, so a man without aspiration cannot rise above his surroundings and become master of his animal inclinations. He is the slave of passions, subject to others, and is carried hither and thither by the changing current of events.

For one to begin to aspire means that he is dissatisfied with his low status, and is aiming at a higher condition. It is a sure sign that he is aroused out of his lethargic sleep of animality, and has become conscious of nobler attainments and a fuller life.

Aspiration makes all things possible. It opens the way to advancement. It brings near and makes real and possible even the highest state of perfection conceivable; that which can be conceived can be achieved.

Aspiration is the twin angel to inspiration. It unlocks the gates of joy. Singing accompanies soaring. Music, poetry, prophecy, and all high and holy instruments are at last placed in the hands of those whose aspirations flag not, whose spirit does not fail.

So long as animal conditions taste sweet to a man, he cannot aspire; he is already satisfied. But when their sweetness turns to bitterness, then in his sorrow he thinks of nobler things. When he is deprived of earthly joy, he aspires to the joy which is heavenly. It is when impurity turns to suffering that purity is sought. Truly, aspiration rises, phoenix-like, from the dead ashes of repentance, but on its powerful pinions man can reach the heaven of heavens.

The man of aspiration has entered the way which ends in peace, and surely he will reach that end if he neither stays nor turns back. If he constantly renews his mind with glimpses of the heavenly vision, he will reach the heavenly state.

Man attains in the measure that he aspires. His longing to be is the gauge of what he can be. To fix the mind is to foreordain the achievement. As man can experience and know all low things, so he can experience and know all high things. As he has become human, so can he become divine. The turning of the mind in high and divine directions is the sole and needful task.

What is impurity but the impure thoughts of the thinker? What is purity but the pure thoughts of the thinker? One man does not do the thinking of another. Each man is pure or impure of himself alone.

If a man thinks, "It is through others, or circumstances, or heredity that I am impure," how can he hope to overcome his errors? Such a thought will check all holy aspirations and bind him to the slavery of passion.

When a man fully perceives that his errors and impurities are his own, that they are generated and fostered by himself, that he alone is responsible for them, then he will aspire to overcome them. The way of attainment will be opened up to him, and he will see from where and to what destination he is travelling.

The man of passion sees no straight path before him, and behind him is all fog and gloom. He seizes the pleasure of the moment and does not strive for understanding or think of wisdom. His way is confused, turbulent and troubled, and his heart is far from peace.

The man of aspiration sees before him the pathway up the heavenly heights, and behind him are the circuitous routes of passion, up which he has hitherto blindly groped. Striving for understanding, and his mind set on wisdom, his way is clear, and his heart already experiences a foretaste of the final peace.

Men of passion strive mightily to achieve little things – things which speedily perish, and, in the place where they were, leave nothing to be remembered.

Men of aspiration strive with equal might to achieve great things – things of virtue, of knowledge, of wisdom, which do not perish, but stand as monuments of inspiration for the uplifting of humankind.

As the merchant achieves worldly success by persistent exertion, so the saint achieves spiritual success by aspiration and endeavour. One becomes a merchant, the other a saint, by the particular direction in which his mental energy is guided.

When the rapture of aspiration touches the mind, it at once refines it, and the dross of its impurities begins to fall away. While aspiration holds the mind, no impurity can enter it, for the impure and the pure cannot at the same moment occupy the thought. But the effort of aspiration is at first spasmatic and short-lived. The mind falls back into its habitual error, and must be constantly renewed.

The lover of the pure life renews his mind daily with the invigorating glow of aspiration. He rises early, and fortifies his mind with strong thoughts and strenuous endeavour. He knows that the mind is of such a nature that it cannot remain unoccupied for a moment, and that if it is not held and guided by high thoughts and pure aspirations, it will assuredly be enslaved and misguided by low thoughts and base desires.

Aspiration can be fed, fostered and strengthened by daily habit, just as is desire. It can be sought, and admitted into the mind as a divine guide, or it can be neglected and shut out. To retire for a short time each day to some quiet spot, preferably in the open air, and there call up the energies of the mind in surging waves of holy rapture, is to prepare the mind for great spiritual victories and destinies of divine import. For such a rapture is the preparation for wisdom and the prelude to peace.

Before the mind can contemplate pure things, it must be lifted up to them, it must rise above impure things; and aspiration is the instrument by which this is accomplished. By its aid the mind soars swiftly and surely into heavenly places, and begins to experience divine things. It begins to accumulate wisdom, and to learn to guide itself by an ever-increasing measure of the divine light of pure knowledge.

To thirst for righteousness, to hunger for the pure life, to rise in holy rapture on the wings of angelic aspiration – this is the right road to wisdom. This is the right striving for peace. This is the right beginning of the way divine.

3

Temptation

Aspiration can carry a man into heaven, but to remain there, he must learn to conform his entire mind to the heavenly conditions. Temptation works to this end.

Temptation is the reversion, in thought, from purity to passion. It is going back from aspiration to desire. It threatens aspiration until the point is reached where desire is quenched in the waters of pure knowledge and calm thought.

In the early stages of aspiration, temptation is subtle and powerful, and is regarded as an enemy; but it is only an enemy in the sense that the one tempted is his own enemy. It is the revealer of weakness and impurity, it is a friend, a necessary factor in spiritual training. It is, indeed, an accompaniment of the effort to overcome evil and apprehend good. To be successfully conquered, the evil in a man must come to the surface and present itself, and it is in temptation that the evil hidden in the heart stands revealed and exposed.

That which temptation appeals to and arouses is unconquered desire, and temptation will again and again assail a man until he has lifted himself above the lusting impulses. Temptation is an appeal to the impure. That which is pure cannot be subject to temptation.

Temptation waylays the man of aspiration until he touches the region of the divine consciousness, and beyond that border, temptation cannot follow him. It is when a man begins to aspire that he begins to be tempted. Aspiration rouses up all the latent good and evil, in order that the man may be fully revealed to himself, for a man cannot overcome himself unless he fully knows himself.

It can scarcely be said of the merely animal man that he is tempted, for the very presence of temptation means that there is a striving for a purer state. Animal desire and gratification is the normal condition of the man who has not yet risen into aspiration. He wishes for nothing more, nothing better, than his sensual enjoyments, and is, for the present, satisfied. Such a man cannot be tempted to fall, for he has not yet risen.

The presence of aspiration signifies that a man has taken one step, at least, upward, and is therefore capable of being drawn back. This backward attraction is called temptation. The allurements of temptation subsist in the impure thoughts and downward desires of the heart. The object of temptation is powerless to attract when the heart no longer lusts for it. The stronghold of temptation is within a man, not without;

and until a man realizes this, the period of temptation will be prolonged.

While a man continues to run away from outward objects, under the delusion that temptation subsists entirely in them, and does not attack and purge away his impure imaginings, his temptations will increase, and his falls will be many and grievous. When a man clearly perceives that the evil is within and not without, then his progress will be rapid, his temptations will decrease, and the final overcoming of all temptation will be well within the range of his spiritual vision.

Temptation is torment. It is not an abiding condition, but is a passage from a lower condition to a higher. The fullness and perfection of life is bliss, not torment. Temptation accompanies weakness and defeat, but a man is destined for strength and victory. The presence of torment is the signal to rise and conquer. The man of persistent and ever renewed aspiration does not allow himself to think that temptation cannot be overcome. He is determined to be master of himself. Resignation to evil is an acknowledgment of defeat. It signifies that the battle against self is abandoned, that good is denied, that evil is made supreme.

As the energetic man of business is not daunted by difficulties but studies how to overcome them, so the man of ceaseless aspiration is not crushed into submission by temptations, but meditates how he may fortify his mind. For the tempter is like a coward, only creeping in at weak and unguarded points.

The tempted one should study thoughtfully the nature and meaning of temptation, for until it is known, it cannot be overcome. A wise general, before attacking the opposing force, studies the tactics of his enemy. Likewise, he who is to overcome temptation must understand how it arises in his own darkness and error, and must study, by introspection and meditation, how to disperse the darkness and supplant error by truth.

The stronger a man's passions, the fiercer will be his temptations; the deeper his selfishness, the more subtle his temptations; the more pronounced his vanity, the more flattering and deceptive his temptations.

A man must know himself if he is to know the truth. He must not shrink from any revelation which will expose his error. On the contrary, he must welcome such revelations as aids to that self-knowledge which is the handmaid of self-conquest.

The man who cannot endure to have his errors and shortcomings brought to the surface and made known, but tries to hide them, is unfit to walk the highway of truth. He is not properly equipped to battle with and overcome temptation. He who cannot fearlessly face his lower nature cannot climb the rugged heights of renunciation.

Let the tempted one know this: that he himself is both tempter and tempted; that all his enemies are within; that the flatterers which seduce, the taunts which stab, and the flames which burn, all spring from that inner region of ignorance and error in which he has hitherto lived. Knowing this, let him be assured of complete victory over evil. When he is sorely tempted, let him not mourn, but let him rejoice in that his strength is tried and his weaknesses exposed. For he who truly knows and humbly acknowledges his weakness will not be slow in setting about the acquisition of strength.

Foolish men blame others for their lapses and sins, but let the truth-lover blame only himself. Let him acknowledge his complete responsibility for his own conduct and not say, when he falls, this thing, or such and such a circumstance, or that man was to blame. For the most which others can do is to afford an opportunity for our own good or evil to manifest itself. They cannot make us good or evil.

Temptation is at first sore, grievous, hard to be borne, and subtle and persistent is the assailant. But if the tempted one is firm and courageous, and does not give way, he will gradually subdue his spiritual enemy, and will finally triumph in the knowledge of good.

The adverse one is compounded of a man's own lust, selfishness, and pride. When these are put away, evil is seen to be naught, and good is revealed in all-victorious splendor.

4

Transmutation

Midway between the hell of passion and the heaven of peace is the purgatory of transmutation – not a speculative purgatory beyond the grave, but a real purgatory in the human heart. In its separating and purifying fire, the base metal of error is sifted away, and only the clarified gold of truth remains.

When temptation has culminated in sorrow and deep perplexity, then the tempted one, strenuously striving for deliverance, finds that his moral servitude is entirely from himself. Instead of fighting against outer circumstances, he must alter inner conditions. The fight against outer things is necessary at the start. It is the only course which can be adopted at first, because of the prevailing ignorance of mental causation. But it never, of itself, brings about emancipation. What it does bring about is the knowledge of the mental cause of temptation.

This knowledge of the mental cause of temptation leads to the transmutation of thought, and the transmutation of thought leads to deliverance from the bondage of error.

The preliminary fighting is a necessary stage in spiritual development, just as the crying and kicking of a helpless babe is necessary to its growth. But as the crying and kicking is not needed beyond the infant stage, so the fierce struggling with, and falling under temptation ends when the knowledge of mental transmutation is acquired.

The truly wise man, he who is enlightened concerning the source and cause of temptation, does not fight against outward allurements – he abandons all desire for them. Thus, they cease to be allurements, and the power of temptation is destroyed at its source. But this abandonment of unholy desire is not a final process. It is the beginning of a regenerative and transforming power which, when patiently employed, leads to the clear and cloudless heights of spiritual enlightenment.

Spiritual transmutation consists of an entire reversal of the ordinary self-seeking attitude of mind toward people and things, and this reversal brings about an entirely new set of experiences. Thus the desire for a certain pleasure is abandoned, cut off at its source, and not allowed to have any place in the consciousness. But the mental force which that desire represented is not annihilated; it is transferred to a higher region of thought, transmuted into a purer form of energy. The law of conservation of energy prevails universally in the mind as it does in matter, and the force shut off in lower directions is liberated in higher realms of spiritual activity.

Along the saintly way towards the divine life, the midway region of transmutation is the country of sacrifice, the plain of renunciation. Old passions, old ambitions and thoughts, are cast away and abandoned, but only to reappear in some more beautiful, more permanent, more eternally satisfying form.

Valuable jewels, long guarded and cherished, when thrown tearfully into the melting pot, are remolded into new and more perfect adornments. Likewise, the spiritual alchemist, at first reluctant to part company with long-cherished thoughts and habits, at last gives them up to discover, a little later, to his joy, that they come back to him in the form of new facilities, rarer powers and purer joys – spiritual jewels newly polished, beautiful, and resplendent.

In transmuting his mind from evil to good, a man comes to distinguish more and more clearly between error and truth, and so distinguishing, he ceases to be swayed and prompted by outward things and by the actions and attitudes of others. Instead, he acts from his knowledge of truth. First acknowledging his errors, and then confronting them with a searching mind and a humble heart, he subdues, conquers, and transmutes them.

The early stage of transmutation is painful but brief, for the pain is soon transformed into pure spiritual joy, the brevity of the pain being measured by the intelligence and energy with which the process is pursued.

While a man thinks that the cause of his pain is in the attitude of others, he will not pass beyond it. But when he perceives that its cause is in himself, then he will pass beyond it into joy.

The unenlightened man allows himself to be disturbed, wounded, and overthrown by what he regards as the wrong attitude of others towards him. This is because the same wrong attitude is in himself. He, indeed, doles out to them, in return, the same actions, regarding as right in himself that which is wrong in others. Slander is given for slander, hatred for hatred, anger for anger. This is the action and reaction of evil. It is the clash of selfishness with selfishness. It is only the self, or selfish elements, within a man that can be aroused by the evil in another. The truth, or divine characteristics in a man cannot be approached by that evil, much less can it be disturbed and overthrown by it.

It is the conversion, or complete reversal of this self or selfishness into truth that constitutes transmutation. The enlightened man has abandoned the delusion that the evil in others has power to hurt and subdue him, and he has grasped the profound truth that he is only overthrown by the evil in himself. He therefore ceases to blame others for his sins and sufferings, and applies himself to purifying his own heart. In this reversal of his mental attitude, he transmutes the lower selfish forces into the higher moral attributes. The base ore of error is cast into the fire of sacrifice, and there comes forth the pure gold of truth.

Such a man stands firm and unmoved when assailed by outward things. He is self's master, not its slave. He has ceased to identify himself with the impulses of passion, and has identified himself with Truth. He has overcome evil, and has become merged in good. He knows both error and truth, and has abandoned error and brought himself into harmony with truth. He returns good for evil. The more he is assailed by evil from without, the greater is his opportunity of manifesting the good from within.

That which supremely differentiates the fool from the wise man is this – that the fool meets passion with passion, hatred with hatred, and returns evil for evil; whereas the wise man meets passion with peace, hatred with love, and returns good for evil.

Men inflict suffering upon themselves through the active instrumentality of their own unpurified nature. They rise into perfect peace in the measure that they purify their hearts. The mental energy which men waste in pursuing dark passions is all-sufficient to enable them to reach the highest wisdom when it is turned in the right direction.

As water, when transmuted into steam, becomes a new, more definite and wide-reaching power, so passion, when transmuted into intellectual and moral force, becomes a new life, a new power for the accomplishment of high and unfailing purposes.

Mental forces, like molecular, have their opposite poles or modes of action. Where the negative pole is, is also the positive. Where ignorance is, wisdom is possible. Where passion abounds, peace awaits. Where there is much suffering, much bliss is near. Sorrow is the negation of joy; sin is the opposite of purity; evil is the denial of good. Where there is an opposite, there is that which is opposed. The adverse evil, in its denial of the good, testifies to its presence. The one thing needful, therefore, is the turning around from the negative to the positive; the conversion of the heart from impure desires to pure aspirations; the transmutation of forces of passion into moral powers.

The wise purify their thoughts. They turn from bad deeds and do good deeds. They put error behind them and approach truth. Thus do they rise above the allurements of sin, above the torments of temptation, above the dark world of sorrow, and enter the divine consciousness, the transcendent life.

5

Transcendence

When a man passes from the dark stage of temptation to the more enlightened stage of transmutation, he has become a saint. A saint is one who perceives the need for self-purification, who understands the way of self-purification, and who has entered that way and is engaged in perfecting himself.

But there comes a time in the process of transmutation when, with the decrease of evil and the accumulation of good, there dawns in the mind a new vision, a new consciousness, a new man. When this is reached, the saint has become a sage; he has passed from the human life to the divine life. He is "born again," and there begins for him a new round of experiences. He wields a new power; a new universe opens out before his spiritual gaze. This is the stage of transcendence. This I call the transcendent life.

When there is no more consciousness of sin; when anxiety and doubt, and grief and sorrow, are ended; when lust and animosity, and anger and envy, no more possess the thoughts; when there remains in the mind no vestige of blame towards others for one's own condition, and when all conditions are seen to be good because they are the result of causes, so that no event can afflict the mind, then transcendence is attained. Then the limited personality is outgrown, and the divine life is known; evil is transcended, and good is all-in-all.

The divine consciousness is not an intensification of the human; it is a new form of consciousness. It springs from the old, but it is not a continuance of it. Born of the lower life of sin and sorrow, after a period of painful torment, it yet transcends that life and has no part in it, just as the perfect flower transcends the seed from which it sprang.

As passion is the keynote of the self-life, so serenity is the keynote of the transcendent life. Rising into it, man is lifted above disharmony and disturbance. When perfect good is realized and known, not as an opinion or an idea, but as an experience or a possession, then calm vision is acquired, and tranquil joy abides through all hardships.

The transcendent life is ruled, not by passions, but by principles. It is founded not upon fleeting impulses, but upon abiding laws. In its clear atmosphere, the orderly sequence of all things is revealed, so that there is seen to be no room for sorrow, anxiety or regret.

While men are involved in the passions of self, they burden themselves with cares, and trouble themselves over many things.

Above all else, they trouble over their own little, burdened, pain-stricken personality, being anxious for its fleeting pleasures, for its protection and preservation, and for its eternal safety and continuance. Now in the life that is wise and good all this is transcended. Personal interests are replaced by universal purposes, and all cares, troubles, and anxieties concerning the pleasure and the fate of the personality are dispelled like the feverish dreams of a night.

Passion is blind and ignorant. It sees and knows only its own gratification. Self recognizes no law; its object is to get and to enjoy. The getting is a graduated scale varying from sensual greed, through many subtle vanities, up to the desire for a personal heaven or personal immortality, but it is self still. It is the old sensual craving coming out in a more subtle and deceptive form. It is longing for some personal delight, along with its accompanying fear that delight should be lost forever.

In the transcendent state, desire and dread are ended, and the thirst for gain and the fear of loss are things that are no more. For where the universal order is seen, and where perennial joy in that good is a normal condition, what is there left to desire? What remains to be feared?

He who has brought his entire nature into conformity and harmony with the law of righteousness, who has made his thoughts pure and his deeds blameless, has entered liberty. He has transcended darkness and mortality, and has passed into light and immortality. For the transcendent state is at first a higher order of morality, then a new form of perception, and at last a comprehensive understanding of the universal moral causation.

And this morality, this vision, and this understanding constitute the new consciousness, the divine life.

The transcendent man is he who is above and beyond the dominion of self. He has transcended evil and lives in the practice and knowledge of good. He is like a man who, having long looked upon the world with darkened eyes, is now restored to sight, and sees things as they are.

Evil is an experience, and not a power. If it were an independent power in the universe, it could not be transcended by any being. But though not real as a power, it is real as a condition and an experience, for all experience is of the nature of reality. It is a state of ignorance, of undevelopment and as such it recedes and disappears before the light of knowledge, as the intellectual ignorance of a child vanishes before the gradually accumulating learning, or as darkness dissolves before the rising light.

The painful experiences of evil pass away as the new experiences of good enter into and possess the field of consciousness. And what are the new experiences of good? They are many and beautiful – such as the joyful knowledge of the freedom from sin. They are the absence of remorse and deliverance from all torments of temptation. They are ineffable joy in conditions and circumstances which formerly caused deep affliction, and imperviousness to be hurt by the actions of others. They are great patience and sweetness of character; serenity of mind under all circumstances; and emancipation from doubt, fear, and anxiety. They are freedom from all dislike, envy, and animosity, with the power to feel and act kindly towards those who see fit to constitute themselves as one's enemies or opponents.

They are the divine power to give blessings for curses, and to return good for evil; a deep knowledge of the human heart, with a perception of its fundamental goodness; and insight into the law of moral causation and the mental evolution of beings, with a prophetic foresight of the sublime good that awaits humanity. Above all, they are a glad rejoicing in the limitation and impotency of evil, and in the eternal supremacy and power of good.

All these, and the calm, strong, far-reaching life that these imply and contain, are the rich experiences of the transcendent man, along with all the new and varied resources, the vast powers, the quickened abilities, and enlarged capacities that spring to life in the new consciousness.

Transcendence is surpassing virtue. Evil and good cannot dwell together. Evil must be abandoned, left behind and transcended before good is grasped and known. When good is practiced and fully comprehended, then all the afflictions of the mind are at an end. For that which is accompanied with pain and sorrow in the consciousness of evil is not so accompanied in the consciousness of good.

Whatsoever happens to the good man cannot cause him perplexity or sorrow, for he knows its cause and issue, knows the good which it is ordained to accomplish in himself, and so his mind remains happy and serene. Though the body of the good man may be bound, his mind is free. Though it be wounded and in pain, joy and peace abide within his heart.

A spiritual teacher had a pupil who was apt and earnest. After several years of learning and practice, the pupil one day offered a question for discussion which his master could not answer. After days of deep meditation, the master said to his pupil, "I cannot answer the question which you have asked. Have you any solution to offer?" Whereupon the pupil formulated a reply to the question which he had propounded. The master then said to him: "You have answered that which I could not, and henceforth neither I nor any man can instruct you, for now you are indeed instructed by truth. You have soared, like the kingly eagle, where no man can follow. Your work is now to instruct others. You are no longer the pupil; you have become the master."

In looking back on the self-life which he has transcended, the divinely enlightened man sees all the afflictions of that life as though his schoolmasters were teaching and leading him upward. And in the measure that he penetrated their meaning and lifted himself above them, they departed from him. Their mission to teach him having ended, they left him the triumphant master of the field. For the lower cannot teach the higher; ignorance cannot instruct wisdom; evil cannot enlighten good; nor can the pupil set lessons for the master. That which is transcended cannot reach up to that which transcends. Evil can only teach in its own sphere, where it is regarded as master. In the sphere of good, it has no place and no authority.

The strong traveller on the highway of truth knows no such thing as resignation to evil; he knows only obedience to good. He who submits to evil, saying, "Sin cannot be overcome, and evil must be borne," thereby acknowledges that evil is his master. It is not his master to instruct him, but to bind and oppress him. The lover of good cannot also be a lover of evil, nor can he, for one moment, admit its ascendancy. He elevates and glorifies good, not evil. He loves light, not darkness.

When a man makes truth as his master, he abandons error. As he transcends error, he becomes more like his master, until at last he becomes one with the truth, teaching it, as a master, by his actions, and reflecting it in his life.

Transcendence is not an abnormal condition; it belongs to the orderly process of evolution. Though, as yet, few have reached it, all will come into it in the course of the ages. And he who ascends into it sins no more, sorrows no more, and is no more troubled. Good are his thoughts, good are his actions, and good is the tranquil tenor of his way. He has conquered self, and has submitted to truth. He has mastered evil, and has comprehended good. Henceforth neither men nor books can instruct him, for he is instructed by the supreme good, the spirit of truth.

6
Beatitude

When divine good is practiced, life is bliss. Bliss is the normal condition of the good man. Those outer assaults, harassments, and persecutions which bring such sufferings to others, only serve to heighten his happiness, for they cause the deep fountain of good within him to well up his greater abundance.

To have transcendent virtue is to enjoy transcendent happiness. The beatific blessedness which god holds out is promised to those having the heavenly virtues – to the merciful, the pure at heart, the peacemakers, and so on. The higher virtue does not merely and only lead to happiness; it is happiness. It is impossible for a man of transcendent virtue to be unhappy. The cause of unhappiness must be sought and found in the self-loving elements, and not in the self-sacrificing qualities. A man may have virtue, and be unhappy, but not so if he has divine virtue.

Human virtue is mingled with self, and therefore, with sorrow. But from divine virtue every taint of self has been purged away, and with it every vestige of misery. One comparison will suffice to illustrate this: a man may have the courage of a lion in attack and self-defense (such courage being a human virtue), but he will not thereby be rendered supremely happy.

However, he whose courage is that of the divine kind which enables him to transcend both attack and defense, and to remain mild, serene, and lovable under attack, such a man will thereby be rendered supremely happy. Moreover, his assailant will be rendered more happy, in that a more powerful good will overcome and cast out the fierce and unhappy evil of the other.

The acquisition of human virtue is a great step towards truth. But the divine way transcends it – truth lies upward and beyond.

Doing good in order to gain a personal heaven or personal immortality is human virtue, but it is not unmixed with self, and not emancipated from sorrow. In the transcendent virtues all is good, and good is all, and there is no personal or ulterior aim. Human virtue is imperfect; it is mixed with the baser, selfish elements, and needs to be transmuted. Divine virtue is unblemished and pure; it is complete and perfect in itself.

And what are the transcendent virtues that embody all happiness and joy? They are:

Impartiality; seeing so deeply into the human heart, and into human actions, that it becomes impossible to take sides with one man or one party against the other, and therefore the power to be perfectly just.

Unlimited kindness towards all men, women, and all creatures, whether enemies or friends.

Perfect patience at all times, in all circumstances, and under severest trials.

Profound humility; the total surrender of self; the judging of one's own actions as though they were the actions of another.

Stainless purity of mind and deed. Freedom from all evil thoughts and impure imaginings.

Unbroken calmness of mind, even in the midst of outward strife, or surrounded by the turmoil of many hardships and difficulties.

Abiding goodness of heart; impervious to evil; returning good for evil.

Compassion; deep pity for all creatures and beings in their sufferings. Shielding the weak and helpless; and protecting, out of pity, even one's enemies from injury and slander.

Abounding love towards all living things; rejoicing with the happy and successful, and sympathizing with the sorrowing and defeated.

Perfect peace toward all things. Being at peace with all the world. A profound reconciliation to the divine order of the universe.

Such are the virtues that transcend both vice and virtue. They include all that virtue embodies, while going beyond it into divine truth. They are the fruits of innumerable efforts to achieve; the glorious gifts of him that overcomes. They constitute the ten-jewelled crown prepared for the calm brow of him who has conquered himself. The mind of the sage is adorned with these majestic virtues. By them he is eternally shielded from sin and sorrow, from harm and hurt, from trouble and turmoil. In them he abides in happiness, a blessedness, a bliss, so pure and tranquil, so deep and high, so far transcending all the fleeting excitements of self, as to be unknown and incomprehensible to the self-seeking consciousness.

The sage has conquered passion and has come to lasting peace. As the mighty mountain remains unmoved by the turbulent ocean that beats at its base, so the mind of the sage, towering in lofty virtue, remains unshaken by the tempests of passion which beat unceasingly upon the shores of life. Good and wise, he is evermore happy and serene. Transcendently virtuous, he lives in beatific bliss.

7

Peace

Where passion is, peace is not; where peace is, passion is not. To know this is to master the first letter in the divine language of perfect deeds. To know that passion and peace cannot dwell together is to be well prepared to renounce the lesser and embrace the greater.

Men pray for peace, yet cling to passion. They foster strife, yet pray for heavenly rest. This is ignorance, profound spiritual ignorance. It is not to know the first letter in the alphabet of things divine.

Hatred and love, strife and peace, cannot dwell together in the same heart. Where one is admitted as a welcome guest, the other will be turned away as an unwelcome stranger. He who despises another will be despised by others. He who opposes his fellow man will himself be resisted. He should not be surprised and mourn that men are divided. He should know that he is propagating strife. He should understand his lack of peace.

He is brave who conquers another; but he who conquers himself is supremely noble. He who is victorious over another may, in turn, be defeated; but he who overcomes himself will never be subdued.

Perfect peace is achieved by the way of self-conquest. Man cannot understand it, cannot approach it, until he sees the supreme necessity of turning away from the fierce fighting of things without, and entering the noble warfare against evils within. He who has realized that the enemy of the world is within, and not without; that his own ungoverned thoughts are the source of confusion and strife; that his own unchastened desires are the violators of his peace, and of the peace of the world; such a man is already on the saintly way.

If a man has conquered lust and anger, hatred and pride, selfishness and greed, he has conquered the world. He has slain the enemies of peace, and peace remains with him.

Peace does not fight; is not partisan; has no blatant voice. The triumph of peace is an unassailable silence.

He who is overcome by force is not thereby overcome in his heart; he may be a greater enemy than before. But he who is overcome by the spirit of peace is thereby changed at heart. He that was an enemy has become a friend. Force and strife work upon passions and fears, but love and peace reach and reform the heart.

The pure-hearted and wise have peace in their hearts. It enters into their actions; they apply it in their lives. It is more powerful than strife; it conquers where force would fail. Its wings shield the righteous. Under its protection, the harmless are not harmed. It affords a secure shelter from the heat of selfish struggle. It is a refuge for the defeated, a tent for the lost, and a temple for the pure.

Where peace is practiced and possessed and known, then sin and remorse, grasping and disappointment, craving and temptation, desiring and grieving – all the turbulence and torment of the mind – are left behind in the dark sphere of the self to which they belong, and beyond which they cannot go.

Beyond where these dark shadows move, the radiant plains of divine beatitude bask in eternal light, and to these, the traveller on the high and holy way comes in due time. From the blinding swamps of passion, through the thorny forests of many vanities, across the arid deserts of doubt and despair, he travels on, not turning back nor straying his course. He ever moves toward his sublime destination, until at last he comes, a humble and lowly, yet strong and radiant conqueror, to the beautiful city of peace.

MAN: KING OF MIND, BODY AND CIRCUMSTANCE

Within, around, above, below,
The primal forces burn and brood,
Awaiting wisdom's guidance; lo!
All their material is good:
Evil subsists in their abuse;
Good, in their wise and lawful use.

Foreword

The problem of life consists in learning how to live. It is like the problem of addition or subtraction to the school boy. When mastered, all difficulty disappears, and the problem has vanished. All the problems of life, whether they be social, political, or religious, subsist in ignorance and wrong-living. As they are solved in the heart of each individual, they will be solved in the mass of men. Humanity at present is in the painful stage of learning. It is confronted with the difficulties of its own ignorance. As men learn to live rightly, learn to direct their forces and use their functions and faculties by the light of wisdom, the sum of life will be correctly done, and its mastery will put an end to all the "problems of evil". To the wise, all such problems have ceased.

James Allen

1

The Inner World of Thoughts

Man is the maker of happiness and misery. Further, he is the creator and perpetuator of his own happiness and misery. These things are not externally imposed; they are internal conditions. Their cause is neither deity, nor devil, nor circumstance, but *thought.* They are the effects of deeds, and deeds are the visible side of thoughts. Fixed attitudes of mind determine courses of conduct, and from courses of conduct come those reactions called *happiness* and *unhappiness.* This being so, it follows that to alter the reactive condition, one must alter the active thought. To exchange misery for happiness, it is necessary to reverse the fixed attitude of mind and habitual course of conduct which is the cause of misery, and the reversed effect will appear in the mind and life. A man has no power to be happy while thinking and acting selfishly; he cannot be unhappy while thinking and acting unselfishly. Wheresoever the cause is, there the effect will appear. Man cannot abrogate effects, but he can alter causes. He can purify his nature; he can remould his character. There is great power in self-conquest; there is great joy in transforming oneself.

Each man is circumscribed by his own thoughts, but he can gradually extend their circle; he can enlarge and elevate his mental sphere. He can leave the low, and reach up to the high; he can refrain from harbouring thoughts that are dark and hateful, and can cherish thoughts that are bright and beautiful. As he does this, he will pass into a higher sphere of power and beauty, will become conscious of a more complete and perfect world.

For men live in spheres low or high according to the nature of their thoughts. Their world is as dark and narrow as they conceive it to be, as expansive and glorious as their comprehensive capacity. Everything around them is tinged with the colour of their thoughts.

Consider the man whose mind is suspicious, covetous and envious. How small, mean and drear everything appears to him. Having no grandeur in himself, he sees no grandeur anywhere. Being ignoble himself, he is incapable of seeing nobility in any being. Even his god is a covetous being that can be bribed, and he judges all men and women to be just as petty and selfish as he himself is, so that he sees in the most exalted acts of unselfishness only motives that are mean and base.

Consider again the man whose mind is unsuspecting, generous, magnanimous. How wondrous and beautiful is his world. He is conscious of some kind of nobility in all creatures and beings. He sees men as true, and to him they are true. In his presence, the meanest forget their nature, and for the moment become like himself, getting a glimpse, albeit confused, in that temporary upliftments of a higher order of things, of an immeasurably nobler and happier life.

That small-minded, and this large-hearted, man live in two different worlds, though they be neighbours. Their consciousness embraces totally different principles. Their actions are each the reverse of the other. Their moral insight is contrary. They each look out upon a different order of things. Their mental spheres are separate, and, like two detached circles, they never mingle. The one is in hell, the other in heaven as truly as they will ever be, and death will not place a greater gulf between them than already exists. To the one, the world is a den of thieves; to the other, it is the dwelling-place of gods. The one keeps a revolver handy, and is always on his guard against being robbed or cheated (unconscious of the fact that he is all the time robbing and cheating himself); the other keeps ready a banquet for the best. He throws open his doors to talent, beauty, genius, goodness. His friends are of the aristocracy of character. They have become a part of himself. They are in his sphere of thought, his world of consciousness. From his heart pours forth nobility, and it returns to him tenfold in the multitude of those who love him and do him honour.

The natural grades in human society – what are they but spheres of thought, and modes of conduct manifesting those spheres? The proletariat may rail against these divisions, but he will not alter or affect them. There is no artificial remedy for equalising states of thought having no natural affinity, and separated by the fundamental principles of life. The lawless and the law-abiding are eternally apart, nor is it hatred nor pride that separates them, but states of intelligence and modes of conduct which in the moral principles of things stand mutually unrelated. The rude and ill-mannered are shut out from the circle of the gentle and refined by the impassable wall of their own mentality. Though they may remove this wall by patient self-improvement, they can never scale by a vulgar intrusion. The kingdom of heaven is not taken by violence, but he who conforms to its principles receives the password. The ruffian moves in a society of ruffians; the saint is one of an elect brethren whose communion is divine music. All men are mirrors reflecting according to their own surface. All men, looking at the world of men and things, are looking into a mirror which gives back their own reflection.

Each man moves in the limited or expansive circle of his own thoughts, and everything outside that circle is non-existent to him. He only knows that which he has become. The narrower the boundary, the more convinced is the man that there is no further limit, no other circle. The lesser cannot contain the greater, and he has no means of apprehending the larger minds; such knowledge comes only by growth. The man who moves in a widely extended circle of thought knows all the lesser circles from which he has emerged, for in the larger experience, all lesser experiences are contained and preserved; and when his circle impinges upon the sphere of perfect manhood, when he is fitting himself for company and communion with them of blameless conduct and profound understanding, then his wisdom will have become sufficient to convince him that there are wider circles still beyond of which he is as yet but dimly conscious, or is entirely ignorant.

Men, like school boys, find themselves in standards or classes to which their ignorance or knowledge entitles them. The curriculum of the sixth standard is a mystery to the boy in the first; it is outside and beyond the circle of his comprehension; but he reaches it by persistent effort and patient growth in learning. By mastering and outgrowing all the standards in between, he comes at last to the sixth, and makes its learning his own; and beyond still is the sphere of the teacher. So in life, men whose deeds are dark and selfish, full of passion and personal desire, cannot comprehend those whose deeds are bright and unselfish, whose minds are calm, deep, and pure, but they can reach this higher standard, this enlarged consciousness, by effort in right doing, by growth in thought and moral comprehension. And above and beyond all lower and higher standards stand the teachers of mankind, the cosmic masters, the saviours of the world whom the adherents of the various religions worship. There are grades in teachers as in pupils, and some there are who have not yet reached the rank and position of *Master*, yet, by the sterling morality of their character, are guides and teachers. But to occupy a pulpit or rostrum does not make a man a teacher. A man is constituted a teacher by virtue of that moral greatness which calls forth the respect and reverence of mankind.

Each man is as low or high, as little or great, as base or noble as his thoughts. No more, no less. Each moves within the sphere of his own thoughts, and that sphere is his world. In that world in which he forms his habits of thought, he finds his company. He dwells in the region which harmonises with his particular growth. But he need not perforce remain in the lower worlds. He can lift his thoughts and ascend. He can pass above and beyond into higher realms, into happier habitations. When he chooses and wills, he can break the carapace of selfish thought, and breathe the purer airs of a more expansive life.

2

The Outer World of Things

The world of things is the other half of the world of thoughts. The inner informs the outer. The greater embraces the lesser. Matter is the counterpart of the mind. Events are streams of thought. Circumstances are combinations of thought, and the outer conditions and actions of others in which each man is involved are intimately related to his own mental needs and development. Man is a part of his surroundings. He is not separate from his fellows, but is bound closely to them by the peculiar intimacy and interaction of deeds, and by those fundamental laws of thought which are the roots of human society.

One cannot alter external things to suit his passing whims and wishes, but he can set aside his whims and wishes; he can also alter his attitude of mind towards externals that they will assume a different aspect. He cannot mould the actions of others towards him, but he can rightly fashion his actions towards them. He cannot break down the wall of circumstance by which he is surrounded, but he can wisely adapt himself to it, or find the way out into enlarged circumstances by extending his mental horizon. Things follow thoughts. Alter your thoughts, and things will receive a new adjustment. To reflect truly, the mirror must be true. A warped glass gives back an exaggerated image. A disturbed mind gives a distorted reflection of the world. Subdue the mind, organise and tranquillise it, and a more beautiful image of the universe, a more prefect perception of the world-order will be the result.

Man has all power within the world of his own mind, to purify and perfect it; but his power in the outer world of other minds is subject and limited. This is made plain when we reflect that each finds himself in a world of men and things, a unit amongst myriads of similar units. These units do not act independently and despotically, but responsively and sympathetically. My fellow men are involved in my actions, and they will deal with them. If what I do be a menace to them, they will adopt protective measures against me. As the human body expels its morbid atoms, so the body politic instinctively expurgates its recalcitrant members. Your wrong acts are so many wounds inflicted on this body politic, and the healing of its wounds will be your pain and sorrow. This ethical cause and effect is not different from that physical cause and effect with which the simplest is acquainted. It is but an extension of the same law; its application to the larger body of humanity. No act is aloof. Your most secret deed is invisibly reported, its good being protected in joy, its evil destroyed in pain. There is a great ethical truth in the old fable of "the Book of Life", in which every thought and deed is recorded and judged. It is because your deed belongs to humanity and the universe that you are powerless to avert external effects. But at the same time, you are all-powerful to modify and correct internal causes; and it is also because of this that the perfecting of one's own deeds is man's highest duty and most sublime accomplishment.

The obverse of this truth – that you are powerless to obviate external things and deeds – is that external things and deeds are powerless to injure you. The cause of your bondage as of your deliverance is within. The injury that comes to you through others is the rebound of your own deed, the reflex of your own mental attitude. *They* are the instruments, *you* are the cause. Destiny is ripened deeds. The fruit of life, both bitter and sweet, is received by each man in just measure. The righteous man is free. None can injure him; none can destroy him; none can rob him of his peace. His attitude towards men, born of understanding, disarms their power to wound him. Any injury which they may try to inflict, rebounds upon themselves to their own hurt, leaving him unharmed and untouched. The good that goes from him is his perennial fount of happiness, his eternal source of strength. Its root is serenity, its flower is joy.

The harm which a man sees in the action of another towards him – say, for instance, an act of slander – is not in the act itself, but in his attitude of mind towards it; the injury and unhappiness are created by himself, and subsist in his lack of understanding concerning the nature and power of deeds. He thinks the act can permanently injure or ruin his character, whereas it is utterly void of any such power. The reality is that the deed can only injure or ruin the doer of it. Thinking himself injured, the man becomes agitated and unhappy, and takes great pains to counteract the supposed harm to himself, and these very pains give the slander an appearance of truth, and aid rather than hinder it. All his agitation and unrest is created by his reception of the deed, and not actually by the deed itself. The righteous man has proved this by the fact that the same act has ceased to arouse in him any disturbance. He understands, and therefore ignores it. It belongs to a sphere which he has ceased to inhabit, to a region of consciousness with which he has no longer any affinity. He does not receive the act into himself, the thought of injury to himself being absent. He lives above the mental darkness in which such acts thrive, and they can no more injure or disturb him than a boy can injure or divert the sun by throwing stones at it. It was to emphasise this that Buddha, to the end of his days, never ceased to tell his disciples that so long as the thought "I have been injured," or "I have been cheated," or "I have been insulted," could arise in a man's mind, he had not comprehended the truth.

And as with the conduct of others, so is it with external things – with surroundings and circumstances – in themselves they are neither good nor bad, it is the mental attitude and state of heart that makes them so. A man imagines he could do great things if he were not hampered by circumstances – by want of money, want of time, want of influence, and want of freedom from family ties. In reality, the man is not hindered by these things at all. He, in his mind, ascribes to them a power which they do not possess, and he submits not to them, but to his opinion about them, that is, to a weak element in his nature. The real "want" that hampers him is the *want of the right attitude of mind.* When he regards his circumstances as spurs to his resources, when he sees that his so-called "drawbacks" are the very steps up which he is to mount successfully to his achievement, then his necessity gives birth to invention, and the "hindrances" are transformed into *aids. The man* is the all-important factor. If his mind be wholesome and rightly tuned, he will not whine and whimper over his circumstances, but will rise up, and outgrow them. He who complains of his circumstances has not yet become a man, and necessity will continue to prick and lash him till he rises into manhood's strength, and then she will submit to him. Circumstance is a severe taskmaster to the weak, an obedient servant to the strong.

It is not external things, but our thoughts about them, that bind us or set us free. We forge our own chains, build our own dungeons, take ourselves prisoners; or we loose our bonds, build our own palaces, or roam in freedom through all scenes and events. If I think that my surroundings are powerful to bind me, that thought will keep me bound. If I think that, in my thought and life, I can rise above my surroundings, that thought will liberate me. One should ask of his thoughts, "Are they leading to bondage or deliverance?" and he should abandon thoughts that bind, and adopt thoughts that set free.

If we fear our fellow-men, fear opinion, poverty, the withdrawal of friends and influence, then we are bound indeed, and cannot know the inward happiness of the enlightened, the freedom of the just; but if in our thoughts, we are pure and free, if we see in life's reactions and reverses nothing to cause us trouble or fear, but everything to aid us in our progress, nothing remains that can prevent us from accomplishing the aims of our life, for then we are free indeed.

3

Habit: Its Slavery and its Freedom

Man is subject to the law of habit. Is he then free? Yes, he is free. Man did not make life and its laws; they are eternal; he finds himself involved in them and he can understand and obey them. Man's power does not enable him to make laws of being; it subsists in discrimination and choice. Man does not create one jot of the universal conditions or laws; they are the essential principles of things, and are neither made nor unmade. He discovers, not makes, them. Ignorance of them is at the root of the world's pain. To defy them is folly and bondage. Who is the freer man, the thief who defies the laws of his country or the honest citizen who obeys them? Who, again, is the freer man, the fool who thinks he can live as he likes, or the wise man who chooses to do only that which is right?

Man is, in the nature of things, a being of habit, and this he cannot alter; but he can alter his habits. He cannot alter the law of his nature, but he can adapt his nature to the law. No man wishes to alter the law of gravitation, but all men adapt themselves to it. They use it by bending to it, not by defying or ignoring it. Men do not run up against walls or jump over precipices in the hope that the law will alter for them. They walk alongside walls, and keep clear of precipices.

Man can no more get outside the law of habit, than he can get outside the law of gravitation, but he can employ it wisely or unwisely. As scientists and inventors master the physical forces and laws by obeying and using them, so wise men master the spiritual forces and laws in the same way. While the bad man is the whipped slave of habit, the good man is its wise director and master. Not its *maker,* let me reiterate, nor yet its arbitrary commander, but its self-disciplined user, its master by virtue of knowledge grounded on obedience. He is the bad man whose habits of thought and action are bad. He is the good man whose habits of thought and action are good. The bad man becomes the good man by transforming or transmuting his habits. He does not alter the law; he alters himself and adapts himself to the law. Instead of submitting to selfish indulgences, he obeys moral principles. He becomes the master of the lower by enlisting in the service of the higher. The law of habit remains the same, but he is changed from bad to good by his readjustment to the law.

Habit is *repetition.* Man repeats the same thoughts, the same actions, the same experiences over and over again until they are incorporated with his being, until they are built into his character as part of himself. Faculty is fixed habit. Evolution is mental accumulation. Man, today, is the result of millions of repetitious thoughts and acts. He is not readymade, he becomes, and is still becoming. His character is predetermined by his own choice. He becomes the thought, the act, which he chooses.

Thus each man is an accumulation of thoughts and deeds. The characteristics which he manifests instinctively and without effort are lines of thought and action that have become automatic by long repetition; for it is the nature of habit to become, at last, unconscious, to repeat, as it were, itself without any apparent choice or effort on the part of its possessor; and in due time it takes such complete possession of the individual as to appear to render his will powerless to counteract it. This is the case with all habits, whether good or bad; when bad, the man is spoken of as being the "victim" of a bad habit or a vicious mind; when good, he is referred to as having, by nature, a "good disposition".

All men are, and will continue to be, subject to their own habits, whether they be good or bad – that is, subject to their own reiterated and accumulated thoughts and deeds. Knowing this, the wise man chooses to subject himself to good habits, for such service is joy, bliss, and freedom; while to become subject to bad habits is misery, wretchedness, slavery.

This law of habit is beneficent, for while it enables a man to bind himself to the chains of slavish practices, it enables him to become so fixed in good courses as to do them unconsciously, to instinctively do that which is right, without restraint or exertion, and in perfect happiness and freedom. Observing this automatism in life, men have denied the existence of will or freedom on man's part. They speak of him as being "born" good or bad, and regard him as the helpless instrument of blind forces.

It is true that man is the instrument of mental forces – or, to be more accurate, he is those forces – but they are not blind, and he can direct them, and redirect them into new channels. In a word, he can take himself in hand and reconstruct his habits; for though it is also true that he is born with a given character, that character is the product of numberless lives during which it has been slowly built up by choice and effort, and in this life it will be considerably modified by new experiences.

No matter how apparently helpless a man has become under the tyranny of a bad habit or a bad characteristic, so long as sanity remains, break away from it and become free, replacing it by its opposite good habit. When the good possesses him as the bad formerly did, there will be neither wish nor need to break from that, for its dominance will be perennial happiness, and not perpetual misery.

That which a man has formed within himself, he can break up and re-form when he so wishes and wills; and a man does not wish to abandon a bad habit so long as he regards it as pleasurable. It is when it assumes a painful tyranny over him that he begins to look for a way of escape, and finally abandons the bad for something better.

No man is helplessly bound. The very law by which he has become a self-bound slave, will enable him to become a self-emancipated master. To know this, he has but to act upon it – that is, to deliberately and strenuously abandon the old lines of thought and conduct, and diligently fashion new and better lines. That he may not accomplish this in a day, a week, a month, a year, or five years, should not dishearten and dismay him. Time is required for the new repetitions to become established, and the old ones to be broken up; but the law of habit is certain and infallible, and a line of effort patiently pursued and never abandoned, is sure to be crowned with success. If a bad condition, a mere negation, can become fixed and firm, how much more surely can a good condition, a positive principle, become established and powerful! A man is only powerless to overcome the wrong and unhappy elements in himself *so long as he regards himself as powerless.* If to the bad habit is added the thought "I cannot" the bad habit will remain. Nothing can be overcome till the thought of powerlessness is uprooted and abolished from the mind. The great stumbling-block is not the habit itself, it is *the belief in the impossibility of overcoming it.* How can a man overcome a bad habit so long as he is convinced that it is impossible? How can a man be prevented from overcoming it when he knows that he can, and is determined to do it? The dominant thought by which man has enslaved himself is the thought "I cannot overcome my sins". Bring this thought out into the light, in all its nakedness, and it is seen to be a belief in the power of evil, with its other pole, disbelief in the power of good. For a man to say, or believe, that he cannot rise above wrong-thinking and wrong-doing, is to submit to evil, to abandon and renounce good.

By such thoughts, such beliefs, man binds himself; by their opposite thoughts, opposite beliefs, he sets himself free. A changed attitude of mind changes the character, the habits, the life. Man is his own deliverer. He has brought about his thraldom; he can bring about his emancipation. All through the ages he has looked, and is still looking for an external deliverer, but he still remains bound. The great deliverer is within; he is the spirit of truth; and the spirit of truth is the spirit of good.

Man is not bound by any power outside his own wrong thoughts, and from these he can set himself free. Foremost, the enslaving thoughts from which he needs to be delivered are – "I cannot rise," "I cannot break away from bad habits," "I cannot alter my nature," "I cannot control and conquer myself," "I CANNOT CEASE FROM SIN." All these "cannots" have no existence in the things to which they submit; they exist only in thought.

Such negations are bad thought-habits which need to be eradicated, and in their place should be planted the positive "I can" which should be tended and developed until it becomes a powerful tree of habit, bearing the good and life-giving fruit of right and happy living.

Habit binds us; habit sets us free. Habit is primarily in thought, secondarily in deed. Turn the thought from bad to good, and the deed will immediately follow. Persist in the bad, and it will bind you tighter and tighter; persist in the good, and it will take you into ever-widening spheres of freedom. He who loves his bondage, let him remain bound. He who thirsts for freedom, let him come and be set free.

4

Bodily Conditions

There are scores of distinct schools devoted to the healing of the body; a fact which shows the great prevalence of physical suffering, as the hundreds of religions, devoted to the comforting of men's minds prove the universality of mental suffering. Each of these schools has its place in so far as it is able to relieve suffering, even where it does not eradicate the evil; for with all these schools of healing, the facts of disease and pain remain with us, just as sin and sorrow remain despite of the many religions.

Disease and pain, like sin and sorrow, are too deep-seated to be removed by palliatives. Our ailments have an ethical cause deeply rooted in the mind. I do not infer by this that physical conditions have no part in disease; they play an important part as *instruments*, as factors in the chain of causation. The microbe that carried the black death was the instrument of uncleanliess, and uncleanliness is, primarily, a moral disorder. Matter is visible mind, and that bodily conflict which we call *disease* has a causal affinity to that mental conflict which is associated with sin. In his present human or self-conscious state, man's mind is continually being disturbed by violently conflicting desires, and his body attacked by morbid elements. He is in a state of mental inharmony and bodily discomfort. Animals in their wild and primitive state are free from disease because they are free from inharmony. They are in accord with their surroundings, have no moral responsibility and no sense of sin, and are free from those violent disturbances of remorse, grief, disappointment, etc., which are so destructive of man's harmony and happiness, and their bodies are not afflicted. As man ascends into the divine or cosmic-conscious state, he will leave behind and below him all these inner conflicts, will overcome sin and all sense of sin, and will dispel remorse and sorrow. Being thus restored to mental harmony, he will become restored to bodily harmony, to wholeness, health.

The body is the image of the mind, and in it are traced the visible features of hidden thoughts. The outer obeys the inner, and the enlightened scientist of the future may be able to trace every bodily disorder to its ethical cause in the mentality.

Mental harmony, or moral wholeness, makes for bodily health. I say *makes for it*, for it will not produce it magically – as though one should swallow a bottle of medicine and then be whole and free. But if the mentality is becoming more poised and restful, if the moral stature is increasing, then a sure foundation of bodily wholeness is being laid, the forces are being conserved and are receiving a better direction and adjustment; and even if perfect health is not gained, the bodily derangement, whatever it be, will have lost its power to undermine the strengthened and uplifted mind.

One who suffers in body will not necessarily at once be cured when he begins to fashion his mind on moral and harmonious principles; indeed, for a time, while the body is bringing to a crisis, and throwing off, the effects of former inhamonies, the morbid condition may appear to be intensified. As a man does not gain perfect peace immediately he enters upon the path of righteousness, but must, except in rare instances, pass through a painful period of adjustment; neither does he, with the same rare exceptions, at once acquire perfect health. Time is required for bodily as well as mental readjustment, and even if health is not reached, it will be approached.

If the mind be made robust, the bodily condition will take a secondary and subordinate place, and will cease to have that primary importance which so many give to it. If a disorder is not cured, the mind can rise above it, and refuse to be subdued by it. One can be happy, strong, and useful in spite of it. The statement so often made by health specialists that a useful and happy life is impossible without bodily health is disproved by the fact that numbers of men who have accomplished the greatest works – men of genius and superior talent in all departments – have been afflicted in their bodies, and today there are plenty of living witnesses to this fact. Sometimes the bodily affliction acts as a stimulus to mental activity, and aids rather than hinders its work. To make a useful and happy life dependent upon health, is to put matter before mind, is to subordinate spirit to body.

Men of robust minds do not dwell upon their bodily condition if it be in any way disordered – *they ignore it*, and work on, live on, as though it were not. This ignoring of the body not only keeps the mind sane and strong, but it is the best resource for curing the body. If we cannot have a perfectly sound body, we can have a healthy mind, and healthy mind is the best route to a sound body.

A sickly mind is more deplorable than a disordered body, and it leads to sickliness of body. The mental invalid is in a far more pitiable condition than the bodily invalid. There are invalids (every physician knows them) who only need to lift themselves into a strong, unselfish, happy frame of mind to discover that their body is whole and capable.

Sickly thoughts about oneself, about one's body and food, should be abolished by all who are called by the name of *man*. The man who imagines that the wholesome food he is eating is going to injure him, needs to come to bodily vigour by the way of mental strength. To regard one's bodily health and safety as being dependent on a particular kind of food which is absent from nearly every household, is to court petty disorders. The vegetarian who says he dare not eat potatoes, that fruit produces indigestion, that apples give him acidity, that pulses are poison, that he is afraid of green vegetables and so on, is demoralising the noble cause which he professes to have espoused, is making it look ridiculous in the eyes of those robust meat eaters who live above such sickly fears and morbid self-scrutinies. To imagine that the fruits of the earth, eaten when one is hungry and in need of food, are destructive of health and life is to totally misunderstand the nature and office of food. The office of food is to sustain and preserve the body, not to undermine and destroy it. It is a strange delusion – and one that must react deleteriously upon the body – that possesses so many who are seeking health by the way of diet, the delusion that certain of the simplest, most natural, and purest of viands are *bad of themselves*, that they have in them the elements of death, and not of life. One of these food-reformers once told me that he believed his ailment (as well as the ailments of thousands of others) was caused by eating bread; not by an excess of bread, but by the bread itself; and yet this man's bread food consisted of nutty, home-made, wholemeal loaves. Let us get rid of our sins, our sickly thoughts, our self-indulgences and foolish excesses before attributing our diseases to such innocent causes.

Dwelling upon one's petty troubles and ailments is a manifestation of weakness of character. To so dwell upon them in thought leads to frequent talking about them, and this, in turn, impresses them more vividly upon the mind, which soon becomes demoralised by such petting and pitying. It is as convenient to dwell upon happiness and health as upon misery and disease; as easy to talk about them, and much more pleasant and profitable to do so.

> "Let us live happily then, not hating those who hate us!
> Among men who hate us let us dwell free from hatred!
> Let us live happily then, free from ailments among the ailing!
> Among men who are ailing let us dwell free from ailments!
> Let us live happily then, free from greed among the greedy!
> Among men who are greedy let us dwell free from greed!"

Moral principles are the soundest foundations for health, as well as for happiness. They are the true regulators of conduct, and they embrace every detail of life. When earnestly espoused and intelligently understood, they will compel a man to reorganise his entire life down to the most apparently insignificant detail. While definitely regulating one's diet, they will put an end to squeamishness, food-fear, and foolish whims and groundless opinions as to the harmfulness of foods. When sound moral health has eradicated self-indulgence and self-pity, all natural foods will be seen as they are – nourishers of the body, and not its destroyers.

Thus a consideration of bodily conditions brings us inevitably back to the mind, and to those moral virtues which fortify it with an invincible protection. The morally right are the bodily right. To be continually transposing the details of life from passing views and fancies, without reference to fixed principles, is to flounder in confusion; but to discipline details by moral principles is to see, with enlightened vision, all details in their proper place and order.

For it is given to moral principle alone, in their personal domain, to perceive the moral order. In them alone resides the insight that penetrates to causes, and with them only is the power to at once command all details to their order and place, as the magnet draws and polarises the filings of steel.

Better even than curing the body is to rise above it; to be its master, and not to be tyrannised over by it; not to abuse it, not to pander to it, never to put its claims before virtue; to discipline and moderate its pleasures, and not to be overcome by its pains – in a word, to live in the poise and strength of the moral powers, this, better than bodily cure, is a yet a safe way to cure, and it is a permanent source of mental vigour and spiritual repose.

5

Poverty

Many of the greatest men through all ages have abandoned riches and adopted poverty to better enable them to accomplish their lofty purposes. Why, then, is poverty regarded as such a terrible evil? Why is it that this poverty, which these great men regard as a blessing, and adopt as a bride, should be looked upon by the bulk of mankind as a scourge and a plague? The answer is simple. In one case, poverty is associated with a nobility of mind which not only takes from it all appearance of evil, but which lifts it up and makes it appear good and beautiful, makes it seem more attractive and more to be desired than riches and honour, so much so that seeing the dignity and happiness of the noble mendicant, thousands imitate him by adopting his mode of life. In the other case, the poverty of our great cities is associated with everything that is mean and repulsive – with swearing, drunkenness, filth, laziness, dishonesty and crime. What, then, is the primary evil: is it poverty, or is it sin? The answer is inevitable – it is sin. Remove sin from poverty, and its sting is gone; it has ceased to be the gigantic evil that it appeared, and can even be turned to good and noble ends. Confucius held up one of his poor disciples, Yen-hwui by name, as an example of lofty virtue to his richer pupils, yet "although he was so poor that he had to live on rice and water, and had no better shelter than a hovel, he uttered no complaint. Where this poverty would have made other men discontented and miserable, he did not allow his equanimity to be disturbed." Poverty cannot undermine a noble character, but it can set it off to better advantage. The virtues of Yen-hwui shone all the more bright for being set in poverty, like resplendent jewels set in a contrasting background.

It is common with social reforms to regard poverty as the *cause* of the sins with which it is associated; yet the same reformers refer to the immoralities of the rich as being caused by their riches. Where there is a cause, its effect will appear and were affluence the cause of immorality, and poverty the cause of degradation, then every rich man would become immoral and every poor man would come to degradation.

An evil-doer will commit evil under any circumstances, whether he be rich or poor, or midway between the two conditions. A right doer will do right, no matter how he be placed. Extreme circumstances may help to bring out the evil which is already there awaiting its opportunity, but they cannot cause the evil, cannot create it.

Discontent with one's financial condition is not the same as poverty. Many people regard themselves as poor whose income runs into several hundreds – and in some cases several thousands of pounds a year, combined with light responsibilities. They imagine their affliction to be poverty; their real trouble is covetousness. They imagine their affliction to be poverty; their real trouble is covetousness. They are not made unhappy by poverty, but by the thirst for riches. Poverty is more often in the mind than in the purse. So long as a man thirsts for more money, he will regard himself as poor, and in that sense he is poor, for covetousness is poverty of mind. A miser may be a millionaire, but he is as poor as when he was penniless.

On the other hand, the trouble with so many who are living in indigence and degradation is that they *are* satisfied with their condition. To be living in dirt, disorder, laziness, and swinish self-indulgence, revelling in foul thoughts, foul words and unclean surroundings, and to be satisfied with oneself, is deplorable. Here again, "poverty" resolves itself into a mental condition, and its solution, as a "problem", is to be looked for in the improvement of the individual from within, rather than of his outward condition. Let a man be made clean and alert within, and he will no longer be content with dirt and degradation outside. Having put his mind in order, he will then put his house in order; indeed, both he and others will know that he has put himself right by the fact that he has put his immediate surroundings right. His altered heart shows in his altered life.

There are, of course, those who are neither self-deceived nor self-degraded and yet are poor. Many such are satisfied to remain poor. They are contented, industrious and happy, and desire nothing else; but those among them who are dissatisfied, and are ambitious for better surroundings and greater scope should, and usually do, use their poverty as a spur to the exercise of their talents and energies. By self-improvement and attention to duty, they can rise into the fuller, more responsible life which they desire.

Devotion to duty is, indeed, not only the way out of that poverty which is regarded as restrictive, it is also the royal road to affluence, influence, and lasting joy, yea, even to perfection itself. When understood in its deepest sense it is seen to be related to all that is best and noblest in life. It includes energy, industry, concentrated attention to the business of one's life, singleness of purpose, courage and faithfulness, determination and self-reliance, and that self-abnegation which is the key to all real greatness. A singularly successful man was once asked, "What is the secret of your success?" and he replied, "Getting up at six o' clock in the morning, and minding my own business." Success, honour and influence always come to him who diligently attends to the business of his life, and religiously avoids interfering with the duties of others.

It may here be urged, and is usually so urged, that the majority of those who are in poverty have not the time or opportunity to give themselves to any special work. This is a mistake. Time and opportunity are always at hand, are with everybody at all times. Those of the poor above mentioned, who are content to remain where they are, can always be diligent in their factory labour, and sober and happy in their homes; but those of them who feel that they could better fill another sphere, can prepare for it by educating themselves in their spare time. The hard-worked poor are, above all, the people who need to economise their time and energies; and the youth who wishes to rise out of such poverty, must at the outset put aside the foolish and wasteful indulgences of alcohol, tobacco, sexual vice, late hours at music halls, clubs and gaming parties, and must give his evenings to the improvement of his mind in that course of education which is necessary to his advancement. By this method, numbers of the most influential men throughout history – some of them among the greatest – have raised themselves from the commonest poverty; a fact which proves that the time of necessity is the hour of opportunity, and not as is so often imagined and declared, the destruction of opportunity; that the deeper the poverty, the greater is the incentive to action in those who are dissatisfied with themselves, and are bent upon achievement.

Poverty is an evil or it is not, according to the character and the condition of mind of the one that is in poverty. Wealth is an evil or not, in the same manner. Tolstoy chafed under his wealthy circumstances. To him they were a great evil. He longed for poverty as the covetous long for wealth. Vice, however, is always an evil, for it both degrades the individual who commits it, and is a menace to society. A logical and profound study of poverty will always bring us back to the individual, and to the human heart. When our social reformers condemn vice as they now condemn the rich; when they are as eager to abolish wrong-living as they now are to abolish low wages, we may look for a diminution in that form of degraded poverty which is one of the dark spots on our civilisation. Before such poverty disappears altogether, the human heart will have undergone, during the process of evolution, a radical change. When that heart is purged from covetousness and selfishness; when drunkenness, impurity, indolence and self-indulgence are driven for ever from the earth, then poverty and riches will be known no more, and every man will perform his duties with a joy so full and deep as is yet (except to the few whose hearts are already pure) unknown to men, and all will eat of the fruit of their labour in sublime self-respect and perfect peace.

6

Man's Spiritual Dominion

The kingdom over which man is destined to rule with undisputed sway is that of his own mind and life; but this kingdom, as already shown, is not separate from the universe, is not confined to itself alone. It is intimately related to entire humanity, to nature, to the current of events in which it is, for the time being, involved, and to the vast universe. Thus the mastery of this kingdom embraces the mastery of the knowledge of life; it lifts a man into the supremacy of wisdom, bestowing upon him the gift of insight into human hearts, giving him the power to distinguish between good and evil, also to comprehend that which is above both good and evil, and to know the nature and consequences of deeds.

At present men are more or less under the sway of rebellious thoughts, and the conquest of these is the supreme conquest of life. The unwise think that everything can be mastered, but oneself, and they seek for happiness for themselves and others by modifying external things. The transposing of outward effects cannot bring permanent happiness, or bestow wisdom; the patching and coddling of a sin-laden body cannot produce health and well-being. The wise know that there is no real mastery until the self is subdued, that when oneself is conquered, the subjugation of externals is finally assured, and they find happiness for ever springing up within them, in the calm strength of divine virtue. They put away sin, and purify and strengthen the body by rising superior to the sway of its passions.

Man can reign over his own mind; can be lord over himself. Until he does so reign, his life is unsatisfactory and imperfect. His spiritual dominion is the empire of the mental forces of which his nature is composed. The body has no causative power. The ruling of the body – that is, of appetite and passion – is the discipline of mental forces. The subduing, modifying, redirecting and transmuting of the antagonising spiritual elements within, is the wonderful and mighty work which all men must, sooner or later, undertake. For a long time, man regards himself as the slave of external forces, but there comes a day when his spiritual eyes open, and he sees that he has been a slave this long time to none and nothing but his own ungoverned, unpurified self. In that day, he rises up and ascending his spiritual throne, he no longer obeys his desires, appetites, and passions, as their slave, but henceforth rules them as his subjects. The mental kingdom through which he has been wont to wander as a beggar and a whipped serf, he now discovers is his by right of lordly self control – his to set in order, to organise and harmonise, to abolish its dissensions and painful contradictions, and bring it to a state of peace.

Thus, rising up and exercising his rightful spiritual authority, he enters the company of those kingly ones who in all ages have conquered and attained, who have overcome ignorance, darkness, and mental suffering, and have ascended into truth.

7

Conquest: Not Resignation

He who has undertaken the sublime task of overcoming himself, does not resign himself to anything that is evil; he subjects himself only to that which is good. Resignation to evil is the lowest weakness; obedience to good is the highest power. To resign oneself to sin and sorrow, to ignorance and suffering, is to say in effect, "I give up; I am defeated; life is evil, and I submit." Such resignation to evil is the reverse of religion. It is a direct denial of good; it elevates evil to the position of supreme power in the universe. Such submission to evil shows itself in a selfish and sorrowful life; a life alike devoid of strength against temptation, and of that joy and calm which are the manifestation of a mind that is dominated by good.

Man is not framed for perpetual resignation and sorrow, but for final victory and joy. All the spiritual laws of the universe are with the good man, for good preserves and shields. There are no laws of evil. Its nature is destruction and desolation.

The conscious modification of the character away from evil and towards good, forms, at present, no part in the common course of education. Even our religious teachers have lost this knowledge and practice, and cannot, therefore, instruct concerning it. Moral growth is mostly unconscious, and is brought about by the stress and struggle of life. The time will come, however, when the conscious formation of character will form an important part in the education of youth, and when no man will be able to fill the position of preacher unless he be a man of habitual self-control, unblemished integrity, and exalted purity, so as to be able to give sound instruction in the making of character, which will then be the main feature of religion.

The doctrine herein set forth by the author is the doctrine of conquest over evil; the annihilation of sin; and necessarily the permanent establishment of man in the knowledge of good, and in the enjoyment of perpetual peace. This is the teaching of the masters of religion in all ages. Howsoever it may have been disguised and distorted by the unenlightened, it is the doctrine of all the perfect ones that were, and will be the doctrine of all the perfect ones that are to come. It is the doctrine of truth.

And the conquest is not of an evil without; not of evil men, or evil spirits, or evil things; but of the evil within; of evil thoughts, evil desires, evil deeds; for when every man has destroyed the evil within his own heart, to where in the whole vast universe will anyone be able to point, and say, "There is evil?" In that great day when all men have become good within, all traces of evil will have vanished from the earth; sin and sorrow will be unknown; and there will be universal joy for evermore.

FOUNDATION STONES TO HAPPINESS AND SUCCESS

Within yourselves deliverance must be sought,
Each man his prison makes.
Each hath such lordship as the loftiest ones;
Nay, for with Powers above, around, below,
As with all flesh and whatsoever lives,
Act maketh joy or woe.

Foreword

How does a man begin the building of a house? He first secures a plan of the proposed edifice, and then proceeds to build according to the plan, scrupulously following it in every detail, beginning with the foundation. Should he neglect the beginning – the beginning on a mathematical plan – his labour would be wasted, and his building, should it reach completion without tumbling to pieces, would be insecure and worthless. The same law holds good in any important work; the right beginning and first essential is *a definite mental plan on which to build*.

Nature will have no slipshod work, no slovenliness and she annihilates confusion, or rather, confusion is in itself annihilated. Order, definiteness, purpose eternally prevail, and he who in his operations ignores these mathematical elements at once deprives himself of substantiality, completeness, happiness and success.

James Allen

1

Right Principles

It is wise to know what comes first, and what to do first. To begin anything in the middle or at the end is to make a muddle of it. The athlete who began by breaking the tape would not receive the prize. He must begin by facing the starter and toeing the mark, and even then a good start is important if he is to win. The pupil does not begin with algebra and literature, but with counting and ABC. So in life – the businessmen who begin at the bottom achieve the more enduring success; and the religious men who reach the highest heights of spiritual knowledge and wisdom are they who have stooped to serve a patient apprenticeship to the humbler tasks, and have not scorned the common experiences of humanity, or overlooked the lessons to be learnt from them.

The first things in a sound life and therefore, in a truly happy and successful life – are *right principles*. Without right principles to begin with, there will be wrong practices to follow with, and a bungled and wretched life to end with. All the infinite variety of calculations which tabulate the commerce and science of the world, come out of the ten figures; all the hundreds of thousands of books which constitute the literature of the world, and perpetuate its thought and genius, are built up from the twenty-six letters. The greatest astronomer cannot ignore the ten simple figures. The profoundest man of genius cannot dispense with the twenty-six simple characters. The fundamentals in all things are few and simple: yet without them there is no knowledge and no achievement. The fundamentals, the basic principles in life, or true living, are also few and simple, and to learn them thoroughly, and study how to apply them to all the details of life, is to avoid confusion, and to secure a substantial foundation for the orderly building up of an invincible character and a permanent success; and to succeed in comprehending those principles in their innumerable ramifications in the labyrinth of conduct, is to become a master of life.

The first principles in life are principles of conduct. To name them is easy. As mere words they are on all men's lips, but as fixed sources of action, admitting of no compromise, few have learned them. In this short talk I will deal with only five of these principles. These five are among the simplest of the root principles of life, but they are those that come nearest to everyday life, for they touch the artisan, the businessman, the householder, the citizen at every point. Not one of them can be dispensed with except at severe cost, and he who perfects himself in their application will rise superior to many of the troubles and failures of life, and will come into these springs and currents of thought which flow harmoniously towards the regions of enduring success. The first of these principles is -

DUTY – A much-hackneyed word, I know, but it contains a rare jewel for him who will seek it by assiduous application. The principle of duty means strict adherence to one's own business, and just as strict non-interference in the business of others. The man who is continually instructing others, gratis, how to manage their affairs, is the one who most mismanages his own. Duty also means undivided attention to the matter in hand, intelligent concentration of the mind on the work to be done; it includes all that is meant by thoroughness, exactness and efficiency. The details of duties differ with individuals, and each man should know his own duty better then he knows his neighbour's, and better than his neighbour knows his; but although the working details differ, the principle is always the same. Who has mastered the demands of duty?

HONESTY is the next principle. It means not cheating or overcharging another. It involves the absence of all trickery, lying and deception by word, look, or gesture. It includes sincerity, the saying what you mean, and the meaning of what you say. It scorns cringing policy and shining compliment. It builds up good reputations, and good reputations build up good businesses, and bright joy accompanies well-earned success. Who has scaled the heights of honesty?

ECONOMY is the third principle. The conservation of one's financial resources is merely the vestibule leading towards the more spacious chambers of true economy. It means, as well, the husbanding of one's physical vitality and mental resources. It demands the conservation of energy by the avoidance of enervating self-indulgences and sensual habits. It holds for its follower strength, endurance, vigilance and capacity to achieve. It bestows great power on him who learns it well. Who has realized the supreme strength of economy?

LIBERALITY follows economy. It is not opposed to it. Only the man of economy can afford to be generous. The spendthrift, whether in money, vitality or mental energy, wasted so much on his own miserable pleasures as to have none left to bestow upon others. The giving of money is the smallest part of liberality. There is a giving of thoughts, deeds, sympathy, the bestowing of goodwill, the being generous towards calumniators and opponents. It is a principle that begets a noble, far-reaching influence. It brings loving friends and staunch comrades, and is the foe of loneliness and despair. Who has measured the breadth of liberality?

SELF-CONTROL is the last of these five principles, yet the most important. Its neglect is the cause of vast misery, innumerable failures, and tens of thousands of financial, physical and mental wrecks. Show me the businessman who loses his temper with a customer over some trivial matter, and I will show you a man who, by that condition of mind, is doomed to failure. If all men practised even the initial stages of self-control, anger, with its consuming and destroying fire, would be unknown. The lessons of patience, purity, gentleness, kindness and steadfastness, which are contained in the principle of self-control, are slowly learned by men, yet until they are truly learned a man's character and success are uncertain and insecure. Where is the man who has perfected himself in self-control? Where he may be, he is a master indeed.

The five principles are five practices, five avenues to achievement and five sources of knowledge. It is an old saying and a good rule that "Practice makes perfect," and he who would make his own the wisdom which is inherent in those principles, must not merely have them on his lips, they must be established in his heart. To know them and receive what they alone can bring, he must *do* them, and give them out in his actions.

2

Sound Methods

From the five foregoing Right Principles, when they are truly apprehended and practised, will issue *Sound Methods*. Right principles are manifested in harmonious action, and method is to life what law is to the universe. Everywhere in the universe there is the harmonious adjustment of parts, and it is this symmetry and harmony that reveals a cosmos, as distinguished from chaos. So in human life, the difference between a true life and a false, between one purposeful and effective and one purposeless and weak, is one of method. The false life is an incoherent jumble of thoughts, passions, and actions; the true life is an orderly adjustment of all its parts. It is all the difference between a mass of lumber and a smoothly working efficient machine. A piece of machinery in perfect working order is not only a useful, but an admirable and attractive thing; but when its parts are all out of gear, and refuse to be readjusted, its usefulness and attractiveness are gone, and it is thrown on the scrap-heap. Likewise, a life perfectly adjusted in all its parts so as to achieve the highest point of efficiency, is not only a powerful, but an excellent and beautiful thing. On the other hand, a life confused, inconsistent, discordant, is a deplorable exhibition of wasted energy.

If life is to be truly lived, method must enter into, and regulate, every detail of it, as it enters and regulates every detail of the wondrous universe of which we form a part. One of the distinguishing differences between a wise man and a foolish one is that the wise man pays careful attention to the smallest things, while the foolish man slurs over them, or neglects them altogether. Wisdom consists in maintaining things on their right relations, in keeping all things, the smallest as well as the greatest, in their proper places and times. To violate order is to produce confusion and discord, and *unhappiness* is but another name for discord.

The good businessman knows that system is three parts of success, and that disorder means failure. The wise man knows that disciplined, methodical living is three parts of happiness, and that looseness means misery. What is a fool but one who thinks carelessly, acts rashly and lives loosely? What is a wise man but one who thinks carefully, acts calmly and lives consistently?

The true method does not end with the orderly arrangement of the material things and external relations of life; this is but its beginning; it enters into the adjustment of the mind – the discipline of passions, the elimination and choice of words in speech, the logical arrangement of thoughts, and the selection of right actions.

To achieve a life rendered sound, successful and sweet by the pursuance of sound methods, one must begin, not by neglect of the little everyday things, but by assiduous attention to them. Thus the hour of rising is important, and its regularity significant; as also are the timing of retiring to rest, and the number of hours given to sleep. Between the regularity and irregularity of meals, and the care and carelessness with which they are eaten, is all the difference between a good and bad digestion (with all that this applies) and an irritable or comfortable frame of mind, with its train of good or bad consequences, for, attaching to these meal-times and meal-ways are matters of both physiological and psychological significance. The due division of hours for business and for play, not confusing the two, the orderly fitting in of all the details of one's business, times for solitude, for silent thought and for effective action, for eating and for abstinence – all these things must have their lawful place in the life of him whose "daily round" is to proceed with the minimum degree of friction, who is to get the most of usefulness, influence and joy out of life.

But all this is but the beginning of that comprehensive method which embraces the whole life and being. When this smooth order and logical consistency is extended to the words and actions, to the thoughts and desires, then wisdom emerges from folly, and out of weakness comes power. When a man so orders his mind as to produce a beautiful working harmony between all its parts, then he reaches the highest wisdom, the highest efficiency, the highest happiness.

But this is the end; and he who would reach the end must begin at the beginning. He must systematise and render logical and smooth the smallest details of his life, proceeding step by step towards the finished accomplishment. But each step will yield its own particular measure of strength and gladness.

To sum up, method produces that smoothness which goes with strength and efficiency. Discipline is method applied to the mind. It produces that calmness which goes with power and happiness. Method is *working* by rule; discipline is *living* by rule. But working and living are not separate; they are but two aspects of character, of life.

Therefore, be orderly in work; be accurate in speech, be logical in thought. Between these and slovenliness, inaccuracy and confusion, is the difference between success and failure, music and discord, happiness and misery.

The adoption of sound methods of working, acting, thinking – in a word, of *living*, is the surest and safest foundation for sound health, sound success, sound peace of mind. The foundation of unsound methods will be found to be unstable, and to yield fear and unrest even while it appears to succeed, and when its time of failure comes, it is grievous indeed.

3

True Actions

Following on right principles and methods come true actions. One who is striving to grasp true principles and work with sound methods will soon come to perceive that details of conduct cannot be overlooked. That indeed, those details are fundamentally distinctive or creative, according to their nature, and are, therefore, of deep significance and comprehensive importance. That this perception and knowledge of the nature and power of passing actions will gradually open and grow within him as an added vision, a new revelation. As he acquires this insight, his progress will be more rapid, his pathway in life more sure, his days more serene and peaceful; in all things he will go the true and direct way, unswayed and untroubled by the external forces that play around and about him. Not that he will be indifferent to the welfare and happiness of those about him;

that is quite another thing, but he will be indifferent to their opinions, to their ignorance, to their ungoverned passions. By true action, I mean acting rightly towards others, and the right-doer knows that actions in accordance with truth are but for the happiness of those about him, and he will do them even though an occasion may arise when someone near to him may advise or implore him to do otherwise.

True actions may easily be distinguished from false by all who wish so to distinguish in order that they may avoid false action, and adopt true. As in the material world we distinguish things by their form, colour, size, etc., choosing those things which we require, and putting by those things which are not useful to us, so in the spiritual world of deeds, we can distinguish between those that are bad and those that are good by their nature, their aim, and their effect and can choose and adopt those that are good, and ignore those that are bad.

In all forms of progress, *avoidance of the bad* always precedes *acceptance and knowledge of the good,* just as a child at school learns to do its lessons right by having repeatedly pointed out to it how it has done them wrong. If one does not know what is wrong and how to avoid it, how can he know what is right and how to practise it? Bad, or untrue, actions are those that spring from a consideration of one's own happiness only, and ignore the happiness of others, that arise in violent disturbances of the mind and unlawful desires, or that call for concealment in order to avoid undesirable complications. Good or true actions are those that spring from a consideration for others, that arise in calm reason and harmonious thought framed on moral principles or that will not involve the doer in shameful consequences if brought into the full light of day.

The right-doer will avoid those acts of personal pleasure and gratification which by their nature bring annoyance, pain, or suffering to others, no matter how insignificant those actions may appear to be. He will begin by putting away these; he will gain a knowledge of the unselfish and true by first sacrificing the selfish and untrue. He will learn not to speak or act in anger, or envy, or resentment, but will study how to control his mind, and will restore it to calmness before acting; and, most important of all, he will avoid, as he would the drinking of deadly poison, those acts of trickery, deceit, double-dealing, in order to gain some personal profit of advantage, and which lead, sooner or later, to exposure and shame for the doer of them. If a man is prompted to do a thing which he needs to conceal, and which he would not lawfully and frankly defend if it were examined of witness, he should know by that that it is a wrong act and therefore to be abandoned without a further moment's consideration.

The carrying out of this principle of honesty and sincerity of action, too, will further lead him into such a path of thoughtfulness in right-doing as will enable him to avoid doing those things which would involve him in the deceptive practices of other people. Before signing papers, or entering into verbal or written arrangements, or engaging himself to others in any way at their request, particularly if they be strangers, he will first inquire into the nature of the work or undertaking, and thus enlightened, he will know exactly what to do, and will be fully aware of the import of his action. To the right-doer *thoughtlessness* is a crime.

Thousands of actions done with good intent lead to disastrous consequences because they are acts of thoughtlessness, and it is well said "that the way to hell is paved with good intentions." The man of true actions is, above all things, thoughtful: "Be ye therefore wise as serpents and harmless as doves."

The term *thoughtlessness* covers a wide field in the realm of deeds. It is only by increasing in thoughtfulness that a man can come to understand the nature of actions, and can, thereby, acquire the power of *always doing that which is right.* It is impossible for a man to be thoughtful and act foolishly. Thoughtfulness embraces wisdom.

It is not enough that an action is prompted by a good impulse or intention; it must arise in *thoughtful consideration* if it is to be a true action; and the man who wishes to be permanently happy in himself and a power for good to others must concern himself only with true actions. "I did it with the best of intentions," is a poor excuse from one who has thoughtlessly involved himself in the wrong-doing of others. His bitter experience should teach him to act more thoughtfully in the future.

True actions can only spring from a true mind, and therefore while a man is learning to distinguish and choose between the false and the true, he is correcting and perfecting his mind, and is thereby rendering it more harmonious and felicitous, more efficient and powerful. As he acquires the "inner eye" to clearly distinguish the right in all the details of life, and the faith and knowledge to do it, he will realise that he is building the house of his character and life upon a rock which the winds of failure and the storms of persecution can never undermine.

4

True Speech

Truth is known by practice only. Without sincerity, there can be no knowledge of truth; and true speech is the beginning of all sincerity. Truth in all its native beauty and original simplicity consists in abandoning and not doing all those things which are untrue, and in embracing and doing all those things which are true. True speech is therefore one of the elementary beginnings in the life of truth. Falsehood, and all forms of deception, slander and all forms of evil-speaking – these must be totally abandoned and abolished before the mind can receive even a small degree of spiritual enlightenment. The liar and slanderer is lost in darkness; so deep is his darkness that he cannot distinguish between good and evil, and he persuades himself that his lying and evil-speaking are necessary and good, that he is thereby protecting himself and other people.

Let the would-be student of "higher things" look to himself and beware of self-delusion. If he is given to uttering words that deceive, or to speaking evil of others – if he speaks in insincerity, envy, or malice – then he has not yet begun to study higher things. He may be studying metaphysics, or miracles, or psychic phenomena, or astral wonders, he may be studying how to commune with invisible beings, to travel invisibly during sleep, or to produce curious phenomena, he may even study spirituality theoretically and as a mere book study, but if he is a deceiver and a backbiter, the higher life is hidden from him. For the higher things are these – *uprightness, sincerity, innocence, purity, kindness, gentleness, faithfulness, humility, patience, pity, sympathy, self-sacrifice, joy, goodwill, love* – and he who would study them, know them, and make them his own, must *practice* them. There is no other way.

Lying and evil-speaking belong to the lowest forms of spiritual ignorance, and there can be no such thing as spiritual enlightenment while they are practised. Their parents are selfishness and hatred.

Slander is akin to lying, but it is even more subtle, as it is frequently associated with indignation, and by assuming more successfully the appearance of truth, it ensnares many who would not tell a deliberate falsehood. For there are two sides to slander – there is *the making of repeating of it*, and there is *the listening to it and acting upon it*. The slanderer would be powerless without a listener. Evil words require an ear that is receptive to evil in which they may fall, before they can flourish; therefore he who listens to a slanderer, who believes it, and allows himself to be influenced against the person whose character and reputation are defamed, is in the same position as the one who framed or repeated the evil report. The evil-speaker is an active slanderer; the evil-listener is a passive slanderer. The two are co-operators in the propagation of evil.

Slander is a common vice and a dark and deadly one. An evil report begins in ignorance, and pursues its blind way in darkness. It generally takes its rise in a misunderstanding. Someone feels that he or she has been badly treated, and, filled with indignation and resentment, unburdens himself to his friends and others in vehement language, exaggerating the enormity of the supposed offence on account of the feeling of injury by which he is possessed. He is listened to and sympathised with. The listeners, without hearing *the other person's* version of what has taken place, and on no other proof than the violent words of an angry man or woman, become cold in their attitude towards the one spoken against, and repeat to others what they have been told, and as such repetition is always more or less inaccurate, a distorted and altogether untrue report is soon passing from mouth to mouth.

It is because slander is such a common vice that it can work the suffering and injury that it does. It is because so many (not deliberate wrong-doers, and unconscious of the nature of the evil into which they so easily fall) are ready to allow themselves to be influenced against one whom they have hitherto regarded as honourable, that an evil report can do its deadly work. Yet its work is only amongst those who have not altogether acquired the virtue of true speech, the cause of which is a truth-loving mind. When one who has not entirely freed himself from repeating or believing an evil report about another, hears of an evil report about himself, his mind becomes aflame with burning resentment, his sleep is broken and his peace of mind is destroyed. He thinks the cause of all his suffering is in the other man and what that man has said about him, and is ignorant of the truth that *the root and cause of his suffering lies in his own readiness to believe an evil report about another.* The virtuous man who has attained to true speech, and whose mind is sealed against even the appearance of evil-speaking cannot be injured and disturbed about any evil reports concerning himself; and although his reputation may for a time be stained *in the minds of those who are prone to suggestions of evil,* his integrity remains untouched and his character unsoiled; for no one can be stained by the evil deeds of another, but only by his own wrongdoing. And so, through all misrepresentation, misunderstanding, and contumely, he is untroubled and unrevengeful; his sleep is undisturbed, and his mind remains in peace.

True speech is the beginning of a pure, wise and well-ordered life. If one would attain to purity of life, if he would lessen the evil and suffering of the world, let him abandon falsehood and slander in thought and word, let him avoid even the appearance of these things, for there are no lies and slanders so deadly as those which are half-truths, and let him not be a participant in evil-speaking by listening to it. Let him also have compassion on the evil-speaker, knowing how such a one is binding himself to suffering and unrest; for no liar can know the bliss of truth; no slanderer can enter the kingdom of peace.

By the words which he utters is a man's spiritual condition declared; by these also is he finally and infallibly adjudged, for as the divine master of the Christian world has declared, "By thy words shalt thou be justified, and by thy words shalt thou be condemned."

5

Equal-mindedness

To be equally-minded is to be peacefully-minded, for a man cannot be said to have arrived at peace who allows his mind to be disturbed and thrown off balance by occurrences.

The man of wisdom is dispassionate, and meets all things with the calmness of a mind in repose and free from prejudice. He is not a partisan, having put away passion, and he is always at peace with himself and the world, not taking sides nor defending himself, but sympathising with all.

The partisan is so convinced that his own opinion and his own side is right, and all that goes contrary to them is wrong, that he cannot think there is any good in the other opinion and the other side. He lives in a continual fever of attack and defence, and has no knowledge of the quiet peace of an equal mind.

The equal-minded man watches himself in order to check and overcome even the appearance of passion and prejudice in his mind, and by so doing he develops sympathy for others, and comes to understand their position and particular state of mind; and as he comes to understand others, he perceives the folly of condemning them and opposing himself to them. Thus there grows up in his heart a divine charity which cannot be limited, but which is extended to all things that live and strive and suffer.

When a man is under the sway of passion and prejudice, he is spiritually blind. Seeing nothing but good in his own side, and nothing but evil in the other, he cannot see anything as it really is, not even his own side; and not understanding himself, he cannot understand the hearts of others, and thinks it is right that he should condemn them. Thus, there grows up in his heart a dark hatred for those who refuse to see with him and who condemn him in return, he becomes separated from his fellow-men, and confines himself to a narrow torture chamber of his own making.

Sweet and peaceful are the days of the equal-minded man, fruitful in good, and rich in manifold blessings. Guided by wisdom, he avoids those pathways which lead down to hatred and sorrow and pain, and takes those which lead up to love and peace and bliss. The occurrences of life do not trouble him, nor does he grieve over those things which are regarded by mankind as grievous, but which must befall all men in the ordinary course of nature. He is neither elated by success nor cast down by failure. He sees the events of his life arrayed in their proper proportions, and can find no room for selfish wishes or vain regrets, for vain anticipations and childish disappointments.

And how is this equal-mindedness, this blessed state of mind and life, acquired? Only by overcoming one's self, only by purifying one's own heart, for the purification of the heart leads to unbiased comprehension, unbiased comprehension leads to equal-mindedness, and equal-mindedness leads to peace. The impure man is swept helplessly away on the waves of passion; the pure man guides himself into the harbour of rest. The fool says, "I have an opinion". The wise man goes about his business.

6

Good Results

A considerable portion of the happenings of life comes to us without any *direct* choosing on our part, and such happenings are generally regarded as having no relation to our will or character, but as appearing fortuitously; as occurring without a cause. Thus one is spoken of as being lucky, and another unlucky, the inference being that each has received something which he never earned, never caused. Deeper thought, and a clearer insight into life convinces us that nothing happens without a cause, and that cause and effect are always related in perfect adjustment and harmony. This being so, every happening directly affecting us is intimately related to our own will. Character is indeed an effect justly related to a cause having its seat in our consciousness. In a word, involuntary happenings of life are the results of our own thoughts and deeds. This, I admit, is not apparent on the surface; but what fundamental law, even in the physical universe, *is* so apparent? If thought, investigation, and experiment are necessary to the discovery of the principles which relate one material atom to another, even so are they imperative to the perception and understanding of the mode of action which relate one mental condition to another; and such modes, such laws, are known by the right-doer, by him who has acquired an understanding mind by the practice of true actions.

We reap as we sow. Those things which come to us, though not by our own *choosing*, are by our *causing*. The drunkard did not choose the delirium tremens or insanity which overtook him, but he caused it by his own deeds. In this case the law is plain to all minds, but where it is not so plain, it is nonetheless true. Within ourselves is the deep-seated cause of all our sufferings, the spring of all our joys. Alter the inner world of thoughts, and the other world of events will cease to bring you sorrow; make the heart pure, and to you all things will be pure, all occurrences happy and in true order.

"Within yourselves deliverance must be sought,
Each man his prison makes.
Each hath such lordship as the loftiest ones;
Nay, for with Powers above, around, below,
As with all flesh and whatsoever lives,
Act maketh joy or woe."

Our life is good or bad, enslaved or free, according to its causation in our thoughts, for out of these thoughts spring all our deeds, and from these deeds come equitable results. We cannot seize good results violently, like a thief, and claim and enjoy them, but we can bring them to pass by setting in motion the causes within ourselves.

Men strive for money, sigh for happiness, and would gladly possess wisdom, yet fail to secure these things, while they see others to whom these blessings appear to come unbidden. The reason is that they have generated causes which prevent the fulfilment of their wishes and efforts.

Each life is a perfectly woven network of causes and effects, of efforts (or lack of efforts) and results, and good results can only be reached by initiating good efforts, good causes. The doer of true actions, who pursues sound methods, grounded on right principles will not need to strive and struggle for good results; they will be there as the effects of his righteous rule of life. He will reap the fruit of his own actions and the reaping will be in gladness and peace.

This truth of sowing and reaping in the moral sphere is a simple one, yet men are slow to understand and accept it. We have been told by a wise one that "the children of darkness are wiser in their day than the children of light", and who would expect, in the material world, to reap and eat where he had not sown and planted? Or who would expect to reap wheat in the field where he had sown tares, and would fall to weeping and complaining if he did not? Yet this is just what men do in the spiritual field of mind and deed. They do evil, and expect to get good, and when the bitter harvesting comes in all its ripened fullness, they fall into despair, and bemoan the hardness and injustice of their lot, usually attributing it to the evil deeds of others, refusing even to admit the possibility of its cause being hidden in themselves, in their own thoughts and deeds. The children of light – those who are searching for the fundamental principles of right living, with a view to making themselves into wise and happy beings – must train themselves to observe this law of cause and effect in thought, word and deed, as implicitly and obediently as the gardener obeys the law of sowing and reaping. He does not even question the law; he recognises and obeys it. When the wisdom which he instinctively practices in his garden, is practiced by men in the garden of their minds – when the law of the sowing of deeds is so fully recognised that it can no longer be doubted or questioned – then it will be just as faithfully followed by the sowing of those actions which will bring about a reaping of happiness and well-being for all. As the children of matter obey the laws of matter, so let the children of spirit obey the laws of spirit, for the law of matter and the law of spirit are one; they are but two aspects of one thing; the outworking of one principle in opposite directions.

If we observe right principles, or causes, wrong effects cannot possibly accrue. If we pursue sound methods, no shoddy thread can find its way into the web of our life, no rotten brick enter into the building of our character to render it insecure; and if we do true actions, what but good results can come to pass; for to say that good causes can produce bad effects is to say that nettles can be reaped from a sowing of corn.

He who orders his life along the moral lines thus briefly enunciated, will attain to such a state of insight and equilibrium as to render him permanently happy and perennially glad; all his efforts will be seasonally planted; all the issues of his life will be good, and though he may not become a millionaire as indeed he will have no desire to become such – he will acquire the gift of peace, and true success will wait upon him as its commanding master.

Recommended Reading

CHASE YOUR LIFE DREAMS

Alka Dixit

Chase Your Life Dreams is a guide to choosing the right, positive thoughts over the negative ones, to find the true purpose of your life, to create your own destiny, and to lead a meaningful and joyous life.

ISBN: 9789387022829; Price: 199; Pages: 186: Format: Paperback;
Genre: Self-help/ Motivation

LIFE IS WHAT MATTERS

Alka Dixit

Life is What Matters is an incredibly motivating tale of a girl who embraced her imperfections and succeeded in life, against all odds. With mantras for living a better life, this book is a treasure.

ISBN: 9789387022188; Pages: 168; Price: 195/-; Format: Paperback;
Genre: Self-help/ Motivation

Dr. Alka Dixit is a practicing doctor and faculty in a medical college in Delhi NCR. She has been guiding people to live a better life by drawing inspiration from her as well as others' life experiences.

LIVE, LOVE AND LAUGH

Manjit S. Chawla

Live, Love and Laugh is a guide to applying the principles of yoga for understanding the human mind and character. The book is a coming together of the practice of yoga, along with the principles and Practice of the law of attraction, making it a spell-binding read.

While **Manjit Sargam Chawla** works for a nationalized bank, her passion lies in motivational speaking and corporate training.

ISBN: 9789387022775; Price: 250; Pages: 184; Format: Paperback

BECAUSE LIFE IS A GIFT

Disha

This book is a collection of true life stories of people with special abilities, who have turned the tide in their favour, with their sheer determination and will.

They will challenge your notion of the impossible. They will inspire you to live life to the fullest, because life is truly a gift.

Disha is an IIM Calcutta alumna and has spent over a decade with corporate giants like Paytm.com, Yatra.com and Mentor Graphics. She is currently a senior leader with Amazon India.

ISBN: 9789382665250; Pages: 208; Price: 150/-; Format: Paperback; Genre: Motivation